Life or Death

Marriage Covenant to יהוה

Itharey.com

Copyright May 12, 2021 Itharey Publishing

Minor revision August 31, 2022
– edits to images, and other minor changes in text.

Written by
Itharey, Daughter of the Diaspora

Table of Contents

Language Keys 4
The children of Yeshar'Al Married 𐤉𐤄𐤅𐤄 5
Who are the children of Yeshar'Al? (Israelites) 16
   The Seed of Yeshar'Al are the children of Yeshar'Al 18
   The Description 24
   The Curses 30
The Children of Yeshar'Al are the Chosen People . 52
𐤉𐤄𐤅𐤄 Hates the Other Nations 55
Chronicles from Abraham to Jacob 61
Chronicles from Egypt to "Canaan" 67
Back to "Egypt" Again 89
𐤉𐤄𐤅𐤄 will Gather his people & Plead with them .. 103
The Consequences of Not Returning to 𐤉𐤄𐤅𐤄 108
The Nations will be Visited & Punished 116
Glory & No more Tears 120
How to Return Back to 𐤉𐤄𐤅𐤄 133

Language Keys

⊐ 𐤄𐤅𐤄𐤉	Yahuah – the name of the Almighty, meaning "his breathe connects life"
Yeshar'Al	The Proper name of the Israelites, the people of 𐤄𐤅𐤄𐤉. The Israelites were more often called "The children of Israel". The term "Israelite" is not in the original language. The word "Israelite" came from the phrase 𐤉𐤔𐤓𐤀𐤋 𐤁𐤍𐤉 "Baney Yeshar'Al" means - children of Yeshar'Al.
Alah	Translated as "God", but the Manakahthey says "𐤀𐤋𐤄" (Alah). This word means the Almighty being that of a savior.
Almighty	Translated as God from the word Alaheym. 𐤀𐤋𐤄𐤉𐤌 (Alaheym) means Almighty, or plural gods. In referencing 𐤄𐤅𐤄𐤉, it means he has many mighty powers, thus its plural form of 𐤀𐤋𐤄.
Alaheym	Sometimes, the word "Alaheym" was translated as "God". Yahuah was sometimes referred to as Alaheym meaning "Almighty or powerful God.

The children of Yeshar'Al Married 𐤉𐤄𐤅𐤄

A marriage is a covenant or contact. You are bound to another if you engage in a contract to be with them for life until their death. This is done between a man and a woman in the state of matrimony.

> Reminder that 𐤉𐤄𐤅𐤄 is "God's name" in Ancient Hebrew known as Manakahthey. 𐤉𐤄𐤅𐤄 is used instead of God throughout this book to honor him. 𐤉𐤄𐤅𐤄 is pronounced as "Yahuah"

The children of Yeshar'Al engaged in a lifelong contract with the Almighty creator whose name is 𐤉𐤄𐤅𐤄 (Yahuah). This is why sometimes he refers to his people as his wife or a woman. 𐤉𐤄𐤅𐤄 provides for his people as a good husband provides for his wife. If a woman leaves her husband for another man, it is considered adultery which brings the penalty of death, unless he divorced her. This is no different with 𐤉𐤄𐤅𐤄 and how he interacts with his people.

Where is your Bill of Divorce?
ISAIAH 50:1

> *This is what 𐤉𐤄𐤅𐤄 says: "Where is your mother's certificate of divorce with which I sent her away? Or to which of My creditors did I sell you? Look, you were sold for your iniquities,*

> *and for your transgressions your mother was sent away.*

HOSEA 2:

> *16And it shall be at that day, saith 𐤉𐤄𐤅𐤄, that thou shalt call me Ishi; and shalt call me no more Baali.*

In the past, the children of Yeshar'Al served other gods, & cheated on 𐤉𐤄𐤅𐤄

> *7And she shall follow after her lovers, but she shall not overtake them; and she shall seek them, but shall not find them: then shall she say, I will go and return to my first husband; for then was it better with me than now.*
>
> *8For she did not know that I gave her corn, and wine, and oil, and multiplied her silver and gold, which they prepared for Baal.*

We will return back to 𐤉𐤄𐤅𐤄 in a renewed covenant

> *19And I will betroth thee unto me for ever; yea, I will betroth thee unto me in righteousness, and in judgment, and in lovingkindness, and in mercies.*

We will always be married to 𐤉𐤄𐤅𐤄

EZEKIEL 16:

> *59For thus saith 𐤉𐤄𐤅𐤄 ALMIGHTY; I will even deal with thee as thou hast done, which hast despised the oath in breaking the covenant.*

In the verse above, 𐤉𐤄𐤅𐤄 states that he would punish us for our sins "deal with us", but he then continues to state that he would "remember" our covenant.

> *60Nevertheless I will remember my covenant with thee in the days of thy youth, and I will establish unto thee an everlasting covenant. 61Then thou shalt remember thy ways, and be ashamed, when thou shalt receive thy sisters, thine elder and thy younger: and I will give them unto thee for daughters, but not by thy covenant. 62And I will establish my covenant with thee; and thou shalt know that I am 𐤉𐤄𐤅𐤄: 63That thou mayest remember, and be confounded, and never open thy mouth any more because of thy shame, when I am pacified toward thee for all that thou hast done, saith 𐤉𐤄𐤅𐤄 ALMIGHTY.*

Life & Death Marriage Covenant with 𐤉𐤄𐤅𐤄

The marriage covenant with Yeshar'Al is a life & Death one. You can not break the covenant without consequences, even death!

Why would the children of Yeshar'Al enter into such a contract?

<u>Answer</u>: The rewards are great and worth it. Read the chapter called "Glory & No more Tears" for more information.

YESHAR'AL HAS A COVENANT WITH 𐤉𐤄𐤅𐤄 ,

NOT RELIGION

Many Israelites say they don't have a religion & often are misunderstood by this statement. This is because a religion is not the same a covenant, though one may feel bound in both cases to do or not do. *<u>Religion, in modern terms, is a belief system, made up by man with no consequences should it be broken</u>. A covenant is a vow exchange or mutual agreement by more than one party, and it can't be broken without an official divorce.* Only 𐤉𐤄𐤅𐤄 can divorce his people, as he is the husband or Master of the covenant.

The Life & Death of the Covenant

is a Mutual Agreement between 𐤉𐤄𐤅𐤄 and the children of Yeshar'Al with consequences of benefits & curses.

The Consequences of Benefits
DEUTERONOMY 28:13

And 𐤉𐤄𐤅𐤄 shall make thee the head, and not the tail; and thou shalt be above only, and thou shalt not be beneath; **if** *that thou hearken unto the commandments of 𐤉𐤄𐤅𐤄 Almighty, which I command thee this day, to observe and to do them:*

The Consequences of Curses

DEUTERONOMY 28:15

But it shall come to pass, **if** *thou wilt not hearken unto the voice of 𐤉𐤄𐤅𐤄 Almighty, to observe to do all his commandments and his statutes which I command thee this day; that all these curses shall come upon thee, and overtake thee:*

DEUTERONOMY 30:

1And it shall come to pass, when all these things are come upon thee, the blessing and the curse, which I have set before thee, and thou shalt call them to mind among all the nations, whither ࠉࠄࠅࠄ your Alah hath driven thee, 2And shalt return unto ࠉࠄࠅࠄ Almighty, and shalt obey his voice according to all that I command thee this day, thou and thy children, with all thine heart, and with all thy soul; 3That then ࠉࠄࠅࠄ your Alah will turn thy captivity, and have compassion upon thee, and will return and gather thee from all the nations, whither ࠉࠄࠅࠄ your Alah hath scattered thee. 4If any of thine be driven out unto the outmost parts of heaven, from thence will ࠉࠄࠅࠄ your Alah gather thee, and from thence will he fetch thee: 5And ࠉࠄࠅࠄ your Alah will bring thee into the land which thy fathers possessed, and thou shalt possess it; and he will do thee good, and multiply thee above thy fathers.

6And ࠉࠄࠅࠄ your Alah will circumcise thine heart, and the heart of thy seed, to love ࠉࠄࠅࠄ your Alah with all thine heart, and with all thy soul, that thou mayest live. 7And ࠉࠄࠅࠄ your Alah will put all these curses upon thine enemies, and on them that hate thee, which persecuted thee. 8And thou shalt return and obey the voice of ࠉࠄࠅࠄ,

and do all his commandments which I command thee this day. 9And 𐤉𐤄𐤅𐤄 *your Alah will make thee plenteous in every work of thine hand, in the fruit of thy body, and in the fruit of thy cattle, and in the fruit of thy land, for good: for* 𐤉𐤄𐤅𐤄 *will again rejoice over thee for good, as he rejoiced over thy fathers: 10If thou shalt hearken unto the voice of* 𐤉𐤄𐤅𐤄 *Almighty, to keep his commandments and his statutes which are written in this book of the law, and if thou turn unto* 𐤉𐤄𐤅𐤄 *your Alah with all thine heart, and with all thy soul.*

The Choice of Life or Death

11For this commandment which I command thee this day, it is not hidden from thee, neither is it far off. 12It is not in heaven, that thou shouldest say, Who shall go up for us to heaven, and bring it unto us, that we may hear it, and do it? 13Neither is it beyond the sea, that thou shouldest say, Who shall go over the sea for us, and bring it unto us, that we may hear it, and do it? 14But the word is very nigh unto thee, in thy mouth, and in thy heart, that thou mayest do it.

15See, I have set before thee this day life and good, and death and evil; 16In that I command thee this day to love 𐤉𐤄𐤅𐤄 Almighty, to walk in his ways, and to keep his commandments and his statutes and his judgments, that thou mayest live and multiply: and 𐤉𐤄𐤅𐤄 your Alah shall bless thee in the land whither thou goest to possess it. 17But if thine heart turn away, so that thou wilt not hear, but shalt be drawn away, and worship other Alahs, and serve them; 18I denounce unto you this day, that ye shall surely perish, and that ye shall not prolong your days upon the land, whither thou passest over Jordan to go to possess it.

*19I call heaven and earth to record this day against you, that I have set before you life and death, blessing and cursing: therefore **choose life**, that both thou and thy seed may live: 20That thou mayest love 𐤉𐤄𐤅𐤄 Almighty, and that thou mayest obey his voice, and that thou mayest cleave unto him: for he is thy life, and the length of thy days: that thou mayest dwell in the land which 𐤉𐤄𐤅𐤄 sware unto thy fathers, to Abraham, to Isaac, and to Jacob, to give them.*

THIS SUMMARY IS CREATED TO AWAKEN YOU ABOUT _WHO YOU ARE_ AND WHAT IS _REQUIRED_ OF YOU ACCORDING TO THIS COVENANT, AS WELL AS TO WARN YOU OF THE _CONSEQUENCES_ OF BREAKING THE COVENANT YOUR ANCESTORS MADE.

This information should be taught to your children because they need to know who they are and their history. This is the history that we ought to teach to our children and prioritize over American History or World History. If we don't learn about our rebellious forefathers, we will become them once again and not end the cycle of rebellion against 𐤉𐤄𐤅𐤄.

You were named in the covenant & therefore are required to keep it. While, you may think you have a choice to serve & obey 𐤉𐤄𐤅𐤄, you don't, at least not without curses & consequences.

Your Name was written in the Marriage Covenant!

DEUTERONOMY 29:

10 Ye stand this day all of you before ᴌᴌᴌᵛ your Almighty; your captains of your tribes, your elders, and your officers, with all the men of Israel, 11 Your little ones, your wives, and thy stranger that is in thy camp, from the hewer of thy wood unto the drawer of thy water: 12 That thou shouldest enter into covenant with ᴌᴌᴌᵛ Almighty, and into his oath, which ᴌᴌᴌᵛ your Alah maketh with thee this day: 13 That he may establish thee to day for a people unto himself, and that he may be unto thee a Alah, as he hath said unto thee, and as he hath sworn

unto thy fathers, to Abraham, to Isaac, and to Jacob.

14Neither with you only do I make this covenant and this oath; 15But with him that standeth here with us this day before 𐤉𐤄𐤅𐤄 our Almighty, and also with him that is not here with us this day:

In Deuteronomy 29:15, it states that you are in this covenant, if you are of the seed of Yeshar'Al whom the promises & curses obtained to.

As part of our marriage covenant to 𐤉𐤄𐤅𐤄, he commanded our fathers to teach our children the laws in the covenant and their history, so they don't repeat the mistakes of the past & suffer the consequences of the curses.

Now that you know the children of Yeshar'Al are bound to 𐤉𐤄𐤅𐤄. Who are they?

Who are the children of Yeshar'Al? (Israelites)

This question can be answered in two ways. By the curses & by the description that was left behind.

This information is shocking, but other nations will be more shocked when they see "so called black people" suddenly come into power.

MICAH 7:15-17

15According to the days of thy coming out of the land of Egypt will I shew unto him marvellous things.

16The nations shall see and be confounded at all their might: they shall lay their hand upon their mouth, their ears shall be deaf.

17They shall lick the dust like a serpent, they shall move out of their holes like worms of the earth: they shall be afraid of ᵧᵤᵥᵥ our Alah, and shall fear because of thee.

Anyone who is from the "seed" of Yeshar'Al is a child of Yeshar'Al. That should make sense, but if it doesn't, I will continue. This means "appearance does not make you his child or offspring or discount you as one".

You are the children of Yeshar'Al…

<u>not</u> because you look black, but because you are of the seed of the man who was called "Yeshar'Al".

Now that I got that out the way…the children of Yeshar'Al had an appearance and that was that of a so called "black man".

There are 3 Tabs in this article. This one will prove that the seed of Yeshar'Al are the children of Yeshar'Al and the 2nd one will prove the children of Yeshar'Al were "black" in appearance and the 3rd will prove that the people of the Atlantic Slave Trade are in fact the children of Yeshar'Al.

The Seed of Yeshar'Al are the children of Yeshar'Al

THESE ARE THE EVIDENCE THAT APPEARANCES DOESN'T MAKE YOU YESHAR'AL, BUT THE SEED DOES

#1) Fathers produce children, as a fruit tree produces fruit, or as a plant produces flowers. The Manakahthey / Hebrew word for a seed that produces & father are the same: אב (AB) Strong's #1 / #3.

The fruit tree came from a seed that was planted and activated in the ground. The father of an apple is the apple tree. The father of a child is the man that implanted their seed into a womb-man / woman. The seed of a an apple tree was planted in the dirt, but no one says the apple came from the dirt. It was the seed that produced, not the dirt. The dirt was the place of growth.

A man that didn't activate a seed inside a woman is never a father, though he may lay with the woman. A father is one who produces children. You are who your father is.

AB = Fruit tree / Father

Father

(Produces children) = 𝒈𝒙 (AB)

Fruit Tree

(Produces fruit) = 𝒈𝒙 (AB)

The fruit tree and father are a thing that produces "fruit". You are not a father if you do not produce fruit (children, offspring) from your seed, thus the father is called "a producer". Interestingly, vegetables & fruits are called "produce".

You can know the fruit by its tree as you can know the son by its father. This should go out without saying, but some people debate whether the child of a man belongs to his nation if he has a child with a foreign woman. An apple tree produces apples, and an orange tree produces oranges, the ground doesn't change this fact.

Thus, the saying "the apple doesn't fall far from its tree". The tree came first, then the fruit / flowers, this is in Genesis.

#2) Two Wives of Yeshar'Al (Jacob) were not Israelites, but foreigners

Some of the sons of Yeshar'Al were not of Rachael or Leah, but foreigners. Yet the children were counted as "the seed of Yeshar'Al because their father was Yeshar'Al

GENESIS 30:1-12

DAN and NAPHTALI

1And when Rachel saw that she bare Jacob no children, Rachel envied her sister; and said unto Jacob, Give me children, or else I die. 2And Jacob's anger was kindled against Rachel: and he said, Am I in Almighty's stead, who hath withheld from thee the fruit of the womb? 3And she said, Behold my maid Bilhah, go in unto her; and she shall bear upon my knees, that I may also have children by her. 4And she gave him Bilhah her handmaid to wife: and Jacob went in unto her. 5And Bilhah conceived, and bare Jacob a son. 6And Rachel said, Almighty hath judged me, and hath also heard my voice, and hath given me a son: therefore called she his name Dan. 7And Bilhah Rachel's maid conceived again, and bare Jacob a second son. 8And Rachel said, With great wrestlings have I wrestled with my sister, and I have prevailed: and she called his name Naphtali.

GAD and ASHER

9When Leah saw that she had left bearing, she took Zilpah her maid, and gave her Jacob to wife. 10And Zilpah

Leah's maid bare Jacob a son. 11And Leah said, A troop cometh: and she called his name Gad. 12And Zilpah Leah's maid bare Jacob a second son. 13And Leah said, Happy am I, for the daughters will call me blessed: and she called his name Asher.

#3) 𐤉𐤄𐤅𐤄 doesn't see as man "sees"

𐤉𐤄𐤅𐤄 did not choose Yeshar'Al because they were black, but because he made a covenant with Abraham, Isaac and Jacob. You should expect for the Children of Yeshar'Al to look like other nations because 𐤉𐤄𐤅𐤄's people were scattered into other nations.

MICAH 5:7-8

And the remnant of Jacob shall be in the midst of many people as a dew from 𐤉𐤄𐤅𐤄, as the showers upon the grass, that tarrieth not for man, nor waiteth for the sons of men.

8 And **the remnant of Jacob shall be among the Gentiles in the midst of many people** *as a lion among the beasts of the forest, as a young lion among the flocks of sheep: who, if he go through, both treadeth down, and teareth in pieces, and none can deliver.*

PROVERBS 27:19

> *As in water face answereth to face, so the heart of man to man.*

1 SAMUEL 16:7

> *But 𐤉𐤄𐤅𐤄 said unto Samuel, Look not on his countenance, or on the height of his stature; because I have refused him: for 𐤉𐤄𐤅𐤄 seeth not as man seeth; for man looketh on the outward appearance, but 𐤉𐤄𐤅𐤄 looketh on the heart.*

It's not your job to identify Yah's people. His people will answer his call. He is not rescuing his people based on skin color.

DEUTERONOMY 28:64

> *And 𐤉𐤄𐤅𐤄 shall scatter thee among all people, from the one end of the earth even unto the other; and there thou shalt serve other gods, which neither thou nor thy fathers have known, even wood and stone.*

JEREMIAH 16:14

> *Therefore, behold, the days come, saith 𐤉𐤄𐤅𐤄, that it shall no more be said, 𐤉𐤄𐤅𐤄 liveth, that brought up the*

children of Israel out of the land of Egypt;

15 But, 𐤉𐤄𐤅𐤄 liveth, that brought up the children of Israel from the land of the north, & from all the lands whither he had driven them: and I will bring them again into their land that I gave unto their fathers.

Israelites were scattered throughout ALL NATIONS by Slavery & Migration. Also, Israelites had marriages with women from the other nations in the past & present.

What are the chances that a person will look like an Israelite, but is not? The same chance that an Israelite will look like the other nations, but is one.

1 SAMUEL 16:7

But 𐤉𐤄𐤅𐤄 said unto Samuel, Look not on his countenance, or on the height of his stature; because I have refused him: for 𐤉𐤄𐤅𐤄 seeth not as man seeth; for man looketh on the outward appearance, but 𐤉𐤄𐤅𐤄 looketh on the heart.

The Description

The Description of the children of Yeshar'Al is that of people of color & many could pass for Egyptians. The Egyptians were black in appearance. Moses was mistaken for an Egyptian and he was of the Yeshar'Al tribe of Luey. There are many scriptures letting you know that the children of Yeshar'Al were so called "black people". Based on the description of the scriptures below, who are the White people in Israel?

SONG OF SOLOMON 1:5

I am black, but comely, O ye daughters of Jerusalem, as the tents of Kedar, as the curtains of Solomon.

LAMENTATIONS 5:10

Our skin was black like an oven because of the terrible famine.

Dreadlocks

SONG OF SOL 5:11

His head is as the most fine gold, his locks are bushy, and black as a raven.

JUDGES 16:19

19And having lulled him to sleep on her lap, she called a man to shave off the seven braids of his head. In this way she began to subdue him, and his strength left him. 20Then she called out, "Samson, the Philistines are here!"

Egypt passing

EXODUS 2:10

When the child had grown older, she brought him to Pharaoh's daughter, and he became her son. She named him Moses and explained, "I drew him out of the water."

Leprosy

Biblical leprosy is actually vitiligo. Vitiligo is a skin condition in which patches of the skin losing their coloration, melanin or pigmentation. The patches of skin affected become white and usually have sharp margins. The name "leprosy" is very accurate to the appearance, although, now it is called vitiligo.

We can know for sure that Moses and his people were people of color by the stories of their skin turning white. If their skin turned white, what color was it before?

LEVITICUS 13:3

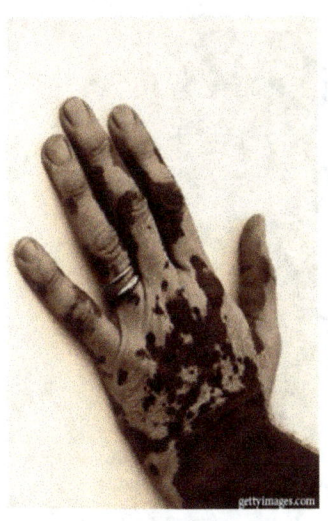

Above Getty image

3 The priest is to examine the infection on his skin, and if the hair in the infection has turned white and the sore appears to be deeper than the skin, it is a skin disease. After the priest examines him, he must pronounce him unclean.

Exodus 4:6

6And 𐤉𐤄𐤅𐤄 said furthermore unto him, Put now thine hand into thy bosom. And he put his hand into his bosom: and when he took it out, behold, his hand was leprous as snow. 7And he said, Put thine hand into thy bosom again. And he put his hand into his bosom again; and plucked it out of his bosom, and, behold, it was turned again as his other flesh.

Numbers 12:9-13

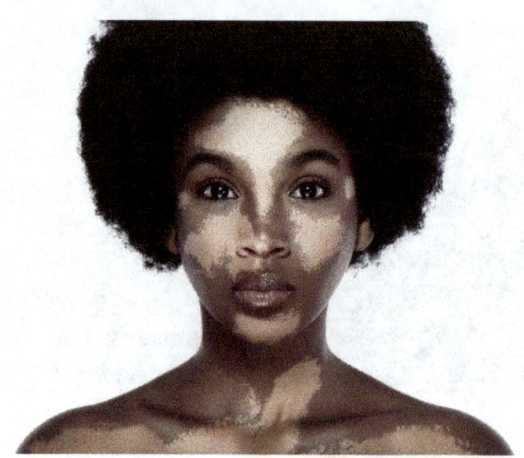

9And the anger of 𐤉𐤄𐤅𐤄 was kindled against them; and he departed. 10And the cloud departed from off the tabernacle; and, behold, Miriam became leprous, white as snow: and Aaron looked upon Miriam, and, behold, she was leprous. 11And Aaron

said unto Moses, Alas, my lord, I beseech thee, lay not the sin upon us, wherein we have done foolishly, and wherein we have sinned. 12Let her not be as one dead, of whom the flesh is half consumed when he cometh out of his mother's womb. 13And Moses cried unto ᴣꟼꟼᵥ, saying, Heal her now, O Al, I beseech thee.

ISAIAH 29:22

Therefore thus saith ᴣꟼꟼᵥ, who redeemed Abraham, concerning the house of Jacob, Jacob shall not now be ashamed, neither shall his face now wax pale.

FAKE JEWS

These people are not the Real Jews. They are all Pale!

These are Israel-Lies or Jew-Wish People

The Curses

JEREMIAH 2:7

And I brought you into a plentiful country, to eat the fruit thereof and the goodness thereof; but when ye entered, ye defiled my land, and made mine heritage an abomination.

All these curses have come upon us because of our own doing. We polluted the land and made our heritage an abomination.

JEREMIAH 17:4

And thou, even thyself, shalt discontinue from thine heritage that I gave thee; and I will cause thee to serve thine enemies in the land which thou knowest not: for ye have kindled a fire in mine anger, which shall burn for ever.

Many so called "black people" don't even know they are the children of Yeshar'Al, this is part of the curse.

We learned in the beginning how the children of Yeshar'Al married 𐤉𐤄𐤅𐤄 and entered in a contract. The curses are upon the children of Yeshar'Al you can even identify us by the curses that came upon us. The curses should be taken as a warning to not break the covenant and return back to 𐤉𐤄𐤅𐤄. It is being used to show you who the children of Yeshar'Al are.

There are two ways in which the curses scattered the children of Yeshar'Al. One is by being scattered and the other was dispersed by Exile & Slavery. The 10 Tribes of Yeshar'Al was scattered and then the remaining tribes of Judah, Benjamin & Levi followed, they were called "The dispersed of Judah". 95% of the slave trade happened to those of Judah, they went to South America! Judah is an Afro-Latino or Loso African Black Portuguese.

Deuteronomy 28 prophesied that the children of Yeshar'Al would be dispersed and scattered if they disobeyed 𐤉𐤄𐤅𐤄 and break their covenant with him. This eventually happened and the curses prove who we are because we are the people of the Atlantic slave trade, the people of the diaspora. This is why I am called "Itharey, daughter of the diaspora". My ancestors were what is now known as "black Spanish Jews". We are exiled and shipped to Cabo Verde and many were taken to the south as it is written in Obadiah.

OBADIAH 1:20

> *And the captivity of this host of the children of Israel shall possess that of the Canaanites, even unto Zarephath; and the captivity of Jerusalem, which is in Sepharad, shall possess the cities of the south.*

The ***Scattered*** Israelites

> The 10 Tribes of Yeshar'Al

The ***Dispersed*** of Judah

> The 3 Tribes of Yeshar'Al

JOEL 3:6

> *The children also of Judah and the children of Jerusalem have ye sold unto the Grecians, that ye might remove them far from their border.*

JEREMIAH 5:15-17

> *15Lo, I will bring a nation upon you from far, O house of Israel, saith יהוה: it is a mighty nation, it is an ancient nation, a nation whose language thou knowest not, neither understandest what they say.*
>
> *16Their quiver is as an open sepulchre, they are all mighty men.*
>
> *17And they shall eat up thine harvest, and thy bread, which thy sons and thy daughters should eat: they shall eat up thy flocks and thine herds: they shall eat up thy vines and thy fig trees: they shall impoverish thy fenced cities, wherein thou trustedst, with the sword.*

Our Forefathers knew the consequences of disobeying 𐤉𐤄𐤅𐤄, do you?

FREE!

DEUTERONOMY 28:58-59

58 If thou wilt not observe to do all the words of this law that are written in this book, that thou mayest fear this glorious and fearful name, 𐤉𐤄𐤅𐤄 YOUR ALAH; 59 Then 𐤉𐤄𐤅𐤄 will make thy plagues wonderful, and the plagues of thy seed, even great plagues, and of long continuance, and sore sicknesses, and of long continuance.

Itharey.com

DEUTERONOMY 28:60-63

60Moreover he will bring upon thee all the diseases of Egypt, which thou wast afraid of; and they shall cleave unto thee. 61Also every sickness, and every plague, which is not written in the book of this law, them will 𐤉𐤄𐤅𐤄 bring upon thee, until thou be destroyed. 62And ye shall be left few in number, whereas ye were as the stars of heaven for multitude; because thou wouldest not obey the voice of 𐤉𐤄𐤅𐤄 your Alah. 63And it shall come to pass, that as 𐤉𐤄𐤅𐤄 rejoiced over you to do you good, and to multiply you; so 𐤉𐤄𐤅𐤄 will rejoice over you to destroy you, and to bring you to nought; and ye shall be plucked from off the land whither thou goest to possess it.

64 And 𐤉𐤄𐤅𐤄 shall scatter thee among all people, from the one end of the earth even unto the other; and there thou shalt serve other gods, which neither thou nor thy fathers have known, **even wood and stone.**

65 And among these nations shalt thou find no ease, neither shall the sole of thy foot have rest: but 𐤉𐤄𐤅𐤄 shall give thee there a trembling heart, and failing of eyes, and sorrow of mind:

66And thy life shall hang in doubt before thee; and thou shalt fear day and night, and shalt have none assurance of thy life:

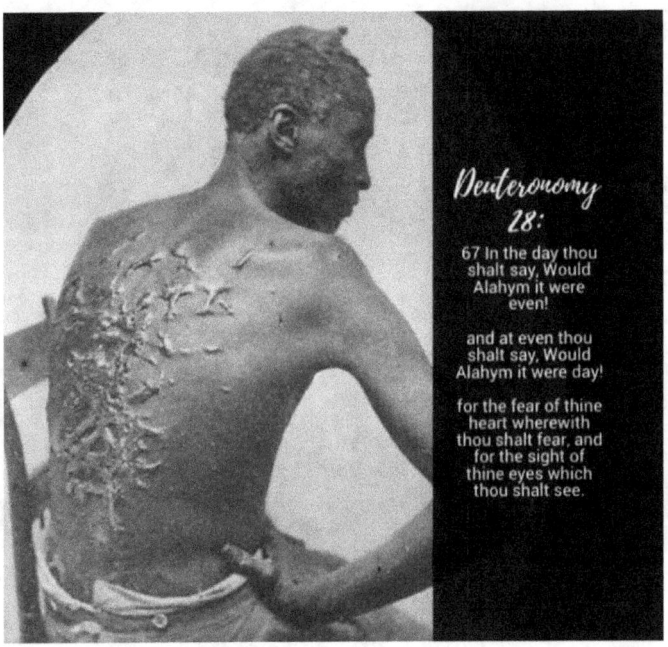

67In the morning thou shalt say, Would it were even! and at even thou shalt say, Would it were morning! for the fear of thine heart wherewith thou shalt fear, and for the sight of thine eyes which thou shalt see.

*68. And יהוה shall bring thee into Egypt again with **ships**, by the way whereof I spake unto thee, Thou shalt see it no more again: and there ye shall be sold unto your enemies for bondmen and bondwomen, and no man shall buy you.*

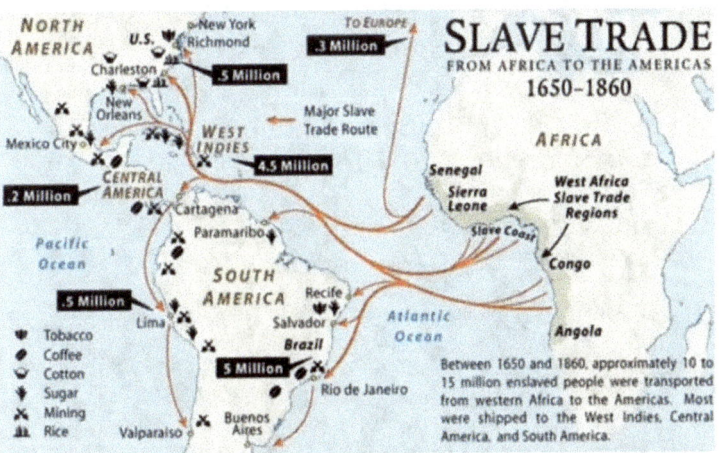

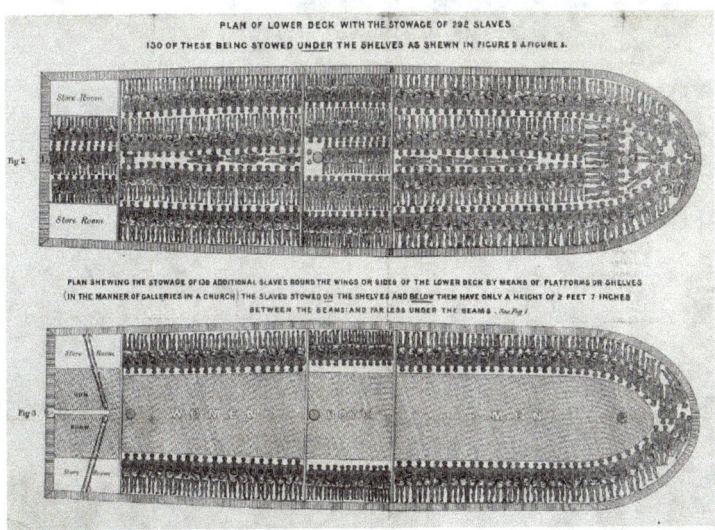

Thou Shalt see it no more again

We fit the description of Deuteronomy 28!

ABOVE IMAGE - 1 RECENTLY BOUGHT SLAVES IN BRAZIL ON THEIR WAY TO THE FARMS OF THE LANDOWNERS WHO BOUGHT THEM C. 1830

TO BE SOLD, on board the Ship *Bance-Island*, on tuesday the 6th of *May* next, at *Asbley-Ferry*; a choice cargo of about 250 fine healthy

NEGROES,

just arrived from the Windward & Rice Coast. —The utmost care has already been taken, and shall be continued, to keep them free from the least danger of being infected with the SMALL-POX, no boat having been on board, and all other communication with people from *Charles-Town* prevented.

Austin, Laurens, & Appleby.

N. B. Full one Half of the above Negroes have had the SMALL-POX in their own Country.

Above image - Spike Gag Mask - cuts the tongue with the slightest movement. This mask stopped slaves from speaking their language of origin & was a torture device

Cursed on the Ships to "Egypt"

Cursed on the Land in "Egypt"

Egypt
= Slavery

INSPECTION AND SALE OF A NEGRO

Research: The Arab Slave Trade!

Strange Family Photos

The Children of Yeshar'Al are the Chosen People

𐤉𐤄𐤅𐤄 choose Yeshar'Al and used us as an example to the other nations. We did not deserve his promise nor do we deserve to be forgiven. For his name sake he will keep his promise which he made to Abraham, Issac & Yeshar'Al. that the Children of Yeshar'Al would be the head and the nations would all serve them

Exodus 32:13

Remember Abraham, Isaac, and Israel, thy servants, to whom thou swarest by thine own self, and saidst unto them, I will multiply your seed as the stars of heaven, and all this land that I have spoken of will I give unto your seed, and they shall inherit it for ever.

Palms 33:12

Blessed is the nation whose Alaheym is 𐤉𐤄𐤅𐤄; and the people whom he hath chosen for his own inheritance.

Deuteronomy 7:6

For thou art an holy people unto 𐤉𐤄𐤅𐤄 your Alah: 𐤉𐤄𐤅𐤄 your Alah hath chosen thee to be a special people unto himself, above all people that are upon the face of the earth.

Deuteronomy 14:2

For thou art an holy people unto 𐤉𐤄𐤅𐤄 your Alah, and 𐤉𐤄𐤅𐤄 hath chosen thee to be a peculiar people unto himself, above all the nations that are upon the earth.

PSALMS 147:19-20

19He sheweth his word unto Jacob, his statutes and his judgments unto Israel.

20He hath not dealt so with any nation: and as for his judgments, they have not known them. Praise ye 𐤉𐤄𐤅𐤄.

ISAIAH 45:4

For Jacob my servant's sake, and Israel mine elect, I have even called thee by thy name: I have surnamed thee, though thou hast not known me.

EXODUS 4:22

And thou shalt say unto Pharaoh, *Thus saith* 𐤉𐤄𐤅𐤄, *Israel is my son, even my firstborn:*

EXODUS 29:45

And I will dwell among the children of Israel, and will be their Alah.

ᎆᏹᎦᏉ Hates the Other Nations

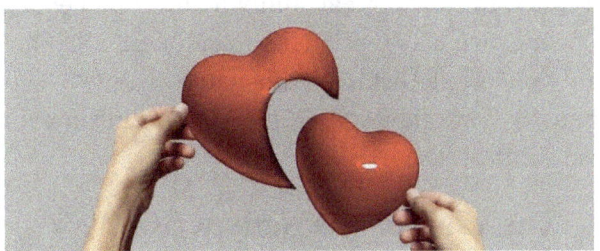

The word hate is strong, but it is a translation of the word ⟨ᎆᏉw "ShaNA"

⟨ᎆᏉw "ShaNA" means to separate from man according to the symbols. Those you abhor, you separate from. This is the word that was translated as "hate". The meaning of "hate" in Manakahthey, is pushing yourself away from the thing you don't like. At anytime, anyone can prays to ᎆᏹᎦᏉ and serve him and he will hear as long as you are righteous. It's not a matter of discrimination based on race, but based on a covenant. He married the children of Yeshar'Al and entered in a covenant with us and we are his "wife" and he just doesn't have a relationship with the other nations.

It is true, ᎆᏹᎦᏉ did indeed separate himself from the other nations and choose the children of Yeshar'Al, however, he did say he loves the Stranger /foreigner who visits the land of Yeshar'Al and he loves those who love him as well as loving the Stranger (those who visit). While these up and coming scriptures appear negative. It is not impartial, but it is specific scriptures that says he hates the nations or thinks low of them. Just know I am not speaking concerning those who are strangers in the land and I am speaking concerning those foreigners who have converted to serving Yah and who love his people. All people are his creation, he made them all. There is only one God /Alah and his name is 𐤉𐤄𐤅𐤄 (Yahuah). Get understanding and don't misinterpret these scriptures.

The Value of the Nations to 𐤉𐤄𐤅𐤄
Psalms 147:

> *19He sheweth his word unto Jacob, his statutes and his judgments unto Israel. 20He hath not dealt so with any nation: and as for his judgments, they have not known them. Praise ye 𐤉𐤄𐤅𐤄.*

Isaiah 40:15

> *Behold, the nations are as a drop of a bucket, and are counted as the small dust of the balance: behold, he taketh up the isles as a very little thing.*

Is this not fair?
Psalms 115:3

> *Our Alah is in heaven; He does as He pleases.*

DANIEL 4:35

*And all the inhabitants of the earth are reputed as **nothing**: and he doeth according to his will in the army of heaven, and among the inhabitants of the earth: and none can stay his hand, or say unto him, What doest thou?*

𐤉𐤄𐤅𐤄 Hated Esau
MALACHI 3:1-4

1 The burden of the word of 𐤉𐤄𐤅𐤄 to Israel by Malachi.

2 I have loved you, saith 𐤉𐤄𐤅𐤄. Yet ye say, Wherein hast thou loved us? Was not Esau Jacob's brother? saith 𐤉𐤄𐤅𐤄: yet I loved Jacob, 3 And I hated Esau, and laid his mountains and his heritage waste for the dragons of the wilderness. 4 Whereas Edom saith, We are impoverished, but we will return and build the desolate places; thus saith 𐤉𐤄𐤅𐤄 of hosts, They shall build, but I will throw down; and they shall call them, The border of wickedness, and, The people against whom 𐤉𐤄𐤅𐤄 hath indignation for ever.

The Nations Were Made to be Servants to The children of Yeshar'Al

GENESIS 9:22-27

22And Ham, the father of Canaan, saw the nakedness of his father, and told his two brethren without. 24And Noah awoke from his wine, and knew what his younger son had done unto him.

25And he said, Cursed be Canaan; **a servant of servants shall he be unto his brethren.** *26And he said, Blessed be 𐤉𐤄𐤅𐤄 (Yahuah) Alaheym of Shem; and* **Canaan shall be his servant**. *27Alaheym shall enlarge Japheth, and he shall dwell in the tents of Shem; and* Canaan shall be his servant.

GENESIS 25:23

And 𐤉𐤄𐤅𐤄 (Yahuah) said unto her,
Two nations are in thy womb,
and two manner of people shall
be separated from thy bowels;
and the one people shall be
stronger than the other people;
and the elder shall serve the
younger

ISAIAH 14:1

For 𐤉𐤄𐤅𐤄 (Yahuah) will have mercy on Jacob, and will yet choose Israel 𐤋𐤀𐤓𐤔𐤉 (YeShaR'AL), and set them in their own land: and the strangers shall be joined with them, and they shall cleave to the house of Jacob.

2 And the people shall take them, and bring them to their place: and the house of Israel 𐤋𐤀𐤓𐤔𐤉 (YeShaR'AL) shall possess them in the land of 𐤉𐤄𐤅𐤄 (Yahuah) for servants and handmaids: and they shall take them captives, whose captives they were; and they shall rule over their oppressors.

ISAIAH 60:11

...that men may bring unto thee the forces of the Gentiles, and that their kings may be brought.

12 For the nation and kingdom that will not serve thee shall perish; yea, those nations shall be utterly wasted.

13 *The glory of Lebanon shall come unto thee, the fir tree, the pine tree, and the box together, to beautify the place of my sanctuary; and I will make the place of my feet glorious.*

14 The sons also of them that afflicted thee shall come bending unto thee; and all they that despised thee shall bow themselves down at the soles of thy feet; and they shall call thee, The city of ᴎᵪᵹᵞ (Yahuah), The Zion of the Holy One of Israel ᒉᵡᵹwᵞ (YeShaR'AL).

Chronicles from Abraham to Jacob

This is the history you should have been taught in school. This is the chronicles of the children of Yeshar'Al began with the promise made to Abraham by 𐤉𐤄𐤅𐤄. This promise was made during his journey to the land of Canaan.

The Promise was Giving to Abraham

Abraham was from the nation of Sham (Shem). Sham was on of Noah's three sons who repopulated the earth. Sham's children would have their own type of culture, traditions and language. However, it didn't happen right away, but through the span of time.

The people from the nation of Sham would be great according to this prophesy.

GENESIS 9:26-27

> *26And he said, Blessed be Master 𐤉𐤄𐤅𐤄 of Shem; and Canaan shall be his servant.*
>
> *27Almighty shall enlarge Japheth, and he shall dwell in the tents of Shem; and Canaan shall be his servant.*

Abraham was from the Nation of Sham through the Ibarey (Hebrew) People

GENESIS 11:10-26

This is the genealogy of Abraham

GENESIS 15:

1Now 𐤉𐤄𐤅𐤄 had said unto Abram, Get thee out of thy country, and from thy kindred, and from thy father's house, unto a land that I will shew thee:

2And I will make of thee a great nation, and I will bless thee, and make thy name great; and thou shalt be a blessing:

3And I will bless them that bless thee, and curse him that curseth thee: and in thee shall all families of the earth be blessed.

4So Abram departed, as 𐤉𐤄𐤅𐤄 had spoken unto him; and Lot went with him: and Abram was seventy and five years old when he departed out of Haran.

Abraham's Promise went to a Chosen Seed – Isaac. Isaac had to be born through Sharah (Sarah), who was chosen too!

GENESIS 17:15-19

15And Alaheym said unto Abraham, As for Sarai thy wife, thou shalt not call her name Sarai, but Sarah shall her name be. 16And I will bless her, and give thee a son also of her: yea, I will bless her, and she shall be a mother of nations; kings of people shall be of her. 17Then Abraham fell upon his face, and laughed, and said in his heart, Shall a child be born unto him that is an hundred years old? and shall Sarah, that is ninety years old, bear? 18And Abraham said unto Alaheym, O that Ishmael might live before thee! 19And Alaheym said, Sarah thy wife shall bear thee a son indeed; and thou shalt call his name Isaac: and I will establish my covenant with him for an everlasting covenant, and with his seed after him.

You are not of chosen seed of Abraham if your great ancestor was not Sharah

Sharah had a son Isaac & he was called the 1st born, even though he wasn't born first. This is because 𐤉𐤄𐤅𐤄 wanted to show it was an election not by birth. Isaac had two sons & Jacob was the chosen seed.

GENESIS 25:20-23

> *20And Isaac was forty years old when he took Rebekah to wife, the daughter of Bethuel the Syrian of Padanaram, the sister to Laban the Syrian. 21And Isaac intreated 𐤉𐤄𐤅𐤄 for his wife, because she was barren: and 𐤉𐤄𐤅𐤄 was intreated of him, and Rebekah his wife conceived. 22And the children struggled together within her; and she said, If it be so, why am I thus? And she went to inquire of 𐤉𐤄𐤅𐤄.*
>
> *23And 𐤉𐤄𐤅𐤄 said unto her, Two nations are in thy womb, and two manner of people shall be separated from thy bowels; and the one people shall be stronger than the other people; and the elder shall serve the younger.*

GENESIS 27:24-29

24And he said, Art thou my very son Esau? And he said, I am. 25And he said, Bring it near to me, and I will eat of my son's venison, that my soul may bless thee. And he brought it near to him, and he did eat: and he brought him wine, and he drank. 26And his father Isaac said unto him, Come near now, and kiss me, my son.

27And he came near, and kissed him: and he smelled the smell of his raiment, and blessed him, and said, See, the smell of my son is as the smell of a field which יהוה hath blessed:

Jacob traveled away from Esau his brother who at this point was trying to kill him for what he did. During his journey he meet an angel who named him Yeshar'Al.

GENESIS 32:24-28

24And Jacob was left alone; and there wrestled a man with him until the breaking of the day. 25And when he saw that he prevailed not against him, he touched the hollow of his thigh; and the hollow of Jacob's thigh was out of joint, as he wrestled with him. 26And he said, Let me go, for the day breaketh. And he said, I will not let thee go, except thou bless me. 27And he said unto him, What is thy name? And he said, Jacob. 28And he said, Thy name shall be called no more Jacob, but Israel: for as a prince hast thou power with Alaheym and with men, and hast prevailed.

Chronicles from Egypt to "Canaan"

𐤉𐤄𐤅𐤄 was with Yeshar'Al & his children throughout their lives. During a great famine, 𐤉𐤄𐤅𐤄 set up Joseph as the 2nd hand of Pharoah to save his people from the famine

GENESIS 47:

> 27So Israel dwelt in the land of Egypt, in the country of Goshen; and they had possessions there and grew and multiplied exceedingly. 28And Jacob lived in the land of Egypt seventeen years. So the length of Jacob's life was one hundred and forty-seven years.

After many years went by, the Egyptians enslaved the children of Yeshar'Al. This was done because 𐤉𐤄𐤅𐤄 hardened the heart of Pharoah in order to show his power to the children of Yeshar'Al.

The land of Canaan is actually the land of Yeshar'Al or Land of Israel. Canaan was the original name of the land named after the first settlers on the land. 𐤉𐤄𐤅𐤄 removed them because they were idol worshipers and the land was promised to Abraham's people, not them. Being the first in something doesn't give you claim to it in the eyes of 𐤉𐤄𐤅𐤄 as may have learned.

We all should know the infamous history of the children of Yeshar'Al who were saved from slavery in Mitsrayim (Egypt). Mitsrayim is the proper name of Egypt.

When the cries from the Israelites in bondage in Mitsrayim came to the Most High 𐤉𐤄𐤅𐤄, he remembered his oaths & promises he made to Abraham, Isaac & Jacab (Yeshar'Al).

as it is written...

EXODUS 13:17-22

> *"23 And it came to pass in process of time, that the king of Mitsrayim died: and the children of Israel sighed by reason of the bondage, and they cried, and their cry came up unto Alahym by reason of the bondage. 24 And Alahym heard their groaning, and Alahym remembered his him master of his house, and ruler of all his substance: 22 To bind his princes at his pleasure; and teach his senators wisdom. 23 Israel also came into Egypt; and Jacob sojourned in the land of Ham. 24 And he increased his people greatly; and made them stronger than their enemies.*

PLAGUES OF MITSRAYIM

25 He turned their heart to hate his people, to deal subtilly with his servants. 26 He sent Moses his servant; and Aaron whom he had chosen. 27 They shewed his signs among them, and wonders in the land of Ham. 028 He sent darkness, and made it dark; and they rebelled not against his word.029 He turned their waters into blood, and slew their fish.030 Their land brought forth frogs in abundance, in the chambers of their kings. 031 He spake, and there came divers sorts of flies, and lice in all their coasts.032 He gave them hail for rain, and flaming fire in their land.033 He smote their vines also and their fig trees; and brake the trees of their coasts. 034 He spake, and the locusts came, and caterpillers, and that without number,035 And did eat up all the herbs in their land, and devoured the fruit of their ground. 036 He smote also all the firstborn in their land, the chief of all their strength.037 He brought them forth also with silver and gold: and there was not one feeble person among their tribes.38 Egypt was glad when they departed: for the fear of them fell upon them.

יהוה Saves the Israelites from Slavery in Mitsrayim (Egypt)"

14 And it shall be when thy son asketh thee in time to come, saying, What is this? that thou shalt say unto him, By strength of hand יהוה brought us out from Mitsrayim, from the house of bondage: 15 And it came to pass, when Pharaoh would hardly let us go, that יהוה slew all the firstborn in the land of Mitsrayim, both the firstborn of man, and the firstborn of beast: therefore I sacrifice to יהוה all that openeth the matrix, being males; but all the firstborn of my children I redeem. 16 And it shall be for a token upon thine hand, and for frontlets between thine eyes: for by strength of hand יהוה brought us forth out of Mitsrayim. 17 And it came to pass, when Pharaoh had let the people go, that Alahym led them not through the way of the

land of the Philistines, although that was near; for Alahym said, Lest peradventure the people repent when they see war, and they return to Mitsrayim. 18 But Alahym led the people about, through the way of the wilderness of the Red sea: and the children of Israel went up harnessed out of the land of Mitsrayim . 19 And Moses took the bones of Joseph with him: for he had straitly sworn the children of Israel, saying, Alahym will surely visit you; and ye shall carry up my bones away hence with you. 20 And they took their journey from Succoth, and encamped in Etham, in the edge of the wilderness. 21 And ﺍﺍﺍﺍ went before them by day in a pillar of a cloud, to lead them the way; and by night in a pillar of fire, to give them light; to go by day and night: 22 He took not away the pillar of the cloud by day, nor the pillar of fire by night, from before the people.

AFTER THE PASSING THROUGH THE RED SEA

PSALMS 105:39

He spread a cloud for a covering; and fire to give light in the night. 40 The people asked, and he brought quails, and satisfied them with the bread of heaven. 41 He opened the rock, and the waters gushed out; they ran in the dry places like a river. 42 For he remembered his set-apart promise, and

> *Abraham his servant. 43 And he brought forth his people with joy, and his chosen with gladness: 44 And gave them the lands of the heathen: and they inherited the labour of the people; 45 That they might observe his statutes, and keep his laws. Praise ye יהוה.*

Yah had very good intentions for the children of Yeshar'Al. His desire was to give them protection, prosperity and the promise land. In return, according to the covenant he made with Abraham, Isaac & Jacob, they would keep his commandments and be holy unto Yah. It's always shocking to read how the Israelites murmured against יהוה after being taking out of Mitsrayim.

ISRAELITES LACKED FAITH IN YAH AFTER BEING SAVED FROM MITSRAYIM

> *10 And when Pharaoh drew nigh, the children of Israel lifted up their eyes, and, behold, the Egyptians marched after them; and they were sore afraid: and the children of Israel cried out unto יהוה. 11 And they said unto Moses, Because there were no graves in Egypt, hast thou taken us away*

todie in the wilderness? wherefore hast thou dealt thus with us, to carry us forth out of Egypt? 12 Is not this the word that we did tell thee in Egypt, saying, Let us alone, that we may serve the Egyptians? For it had been better for us to serve the Egyptians, than that we should die in the wilderness.

-Exodus 14:9-12

WE ARE TO TRUST 𐤉𐤄𐤅𐤄

5 We will rejoice in thy salvation, and in the name of our Alahym we will set up our banners: 𐤉𐤄𐤅𐤄 fulfil all thy petitions. 6 Now know I that 𐤉𐤄𐤅𐤄 savethhis anointed; he will hear him from his set-apart heaven with the saving strength of his right hand. 7 Some trust in chariots, and some in horses: but we will remember the name of 𐤉𐤄𐤅𐤄 our Alahym.

-Psalms 20:5-7

𐤉𐤄𐤅𐤄 GAVE ISRAEL WATER OUT OF A ROCK

PSALMS 78:12

> *Marvellous things did he in the sight of their fathers, in the land of Egypt, in the field of Zoan. 13 He divided the sea, and caused them to pass through; and he made the waters to stand as an heap. 14 In the daytime also he led them with a cloud, and all the night with a light of fire. 15 He clave the rocks in the wilderness, and gave them drink as out of the great depths. 16 He brought streams also out of the rock, and caused waters to run down like rivers. 17 And they sinned yet more against him by provoking the most High in the wilderness. 18 And they tempted El in their heart by asking meat for their lust. 19 Yea, they spake against Alahym; they said, Can El furnish a table in the wilderness?*

𐤉𐤄𐤅𐤄 MADE IT RAIN BREAD & MEAT FOR ISRAEL

20 Behold, he smote the rock, that the waters gushed out, and the streams overflowed; can he give bread also? can he provide flesh for his people? 21 Therefore 𐤉𐤄𐤅𐤄 heard this, and was wroth: so a fire was kindled against Jacob, and anger also came up against Israel;22 Because they believed not in Alahym, and trusted not in his salvation: 23 Though he had commanded the clouds from above, and opened the doors of heaven, 24 And had rained down manna upon them to eat, and had given them of the corn of heaven. 25 Man did eat angels' food: he sent them meat to the full.26 He caused an east wind to blow in the heaven: and by his power he brought in the south wind. 27 He rained flesh also upon them as dust, and feathered fowls like as the sand of the sea: 28 And he let it fall in the midst of their camp, round about their habitations. 29 So they did eat, and were well filled: for he gave them their own desire; 30 They were not estranged from their lust. But while their meat was yet in their mouths, 31 The wrath of Alahym came upon them, and slew the fattest of them, and smote down the chosen men of Israel. 32 For all this they sinned still, and believed not for his wondrous works. 33 Therefore their days did he consume in vanity, and their years in trouble. 34 When he slew them, then they sought him: and they returned and inquired early after El. 35 And they remembered that Alahym was their rock, and El Elyon their redeemer.

IN THE WILDERNESS

PSALMS 106:13-31

They soon forgat his works; they waited not for his counsel: 14 But lusted exceedingly in the wilderness, and tempted El in the desert. 15 And he gave them their request; but sent leanness into their soul. 16 They envied Moses also in the camp, and Aaron the saint of 𐤉𐤄𐤅𐤄. 17 The earth opened and swallowed up Dathan, and covered the company of Abiram. 18 And a fire was kindled in their company; the flame burned up the wicked. 19 They made a calf in Horeb, and worshipped the molten image. 20 Thus they changed their glory into the similitude of an ox that eateth grass.21 They forgat El their saviour, which had done great things in Egypt;22 Wondrous works in the land of Ham, and terrible things by the Red sea. 23 Therefore he said that he would destroy them, had not Moses his chosen stood before him in the breach, to turn away his wrath, lest he should destroy them.24 Yea, they despised the pleasant land, they believed not his word: 25 But murmured in their tents, and hearkened not unto the voice of יהוה. 26 Therefore he lifted up his hand against them, to overthrow them in the wilderness: 27 To overthrow their seed also among the nations, and to scatter them in the lands.28 They joined themselves also unto Baal-peor, and ate the sacrifices of the dead.29 Thus they provoked him to anger with their inventions: and the plague brake in upon them.30 Then stood up Phinehas, and executed judgment: and so the plague was stayed. 31 And that was counted unto him for righteousness unto all generations for evermore.

Psalms 106:6

We have sinned with our fathers, we have committed iniquity, we have done wickedly.

SAVED FROM MIZRIAM

7 Our fathers understood not thy wonders in Egypt; they remembered not the multitude ofthy mercies; but provoked him at the sea, even at the Red sea. 8 Nevertheless he saved them for his name's sake, that he might make his mighty power to be known. 9 He rebuked the Red sea also, and it was dried up: so he led them through the depths, as through the wilderness. 10 And he saved them from the hand of him that hated them, and redeemed them from the hand of the enemy. 11 And the waters covered their enemies: there was not one of them left. 12 Then believed they his words; they sang his praise.

ISRAELITES WERE NEVER SINCERE TO WORSHIP YAH & KEEP HIS COVENANT WITH HIM

PSALMS 78:36

Nevertheless they did flatter him with their mouth, and they lied unto him with their tongues. 37 For their heart was not right with him, neither were they stedfast in his covenant. 38 But he, being full of compassion, forgave their iniquity, and destroyed them not: yea, many a time turned he his anger away, and did not stir up all his wrath. 39 For he remembered that they were but flesh; a wind that passeth away, and cometh not again.

THE ISRAELITES FORGOT YAH'S MIRACLES IN MIZRIAM

PSALMS 78:40

How oft did they provoke him in the wilderness, and grieve him in the desert! 41 Yea, they turned back and tempted El, and limited the Set-apart One of Israel. 42 They remembered not his hand, nor the day when he delivered them from the enemy. 43 How he had wrought his signs in Egypt, and his wonders in the field of

Zoan: 44 And had turned their rivers into blood; and their floods, that they could not drink. 45 He sent divers sorts of flies among them, which devoured them; and frogs, which destroyed them. 46 He gave also their increase unto the caterpiller, and their labour unto the locust. 47 He destroyed their vines with hail, and their sycomore trees with frost. 48 He gave up their cattle also to the hail, and their flocks to hot thunderbolts. 49 He cast upon them the fierceness of his anger, wrath, and indignation, and trouble, by sending evil angels among them. 50 He made a way to his anger; he spared not their soul from death, but gave their life over to the pestilence; 51 And smote all the firstborn in Mitsrayim; the chief of their strength in the tabernacles of Ham: 52 But made his own people to go forth like sheep, and guided them in the wilderness like a flock. 53 And he led them on safely, so that they feared not: but the sea overwhelmed their enemies.

𐤉𐤄𐤅𐤄 DRIVES OUT THE NATIONS & GIVES ISRAEL THE LAND OF CANAAN

PSALMS 78:54

> *And he brought them to the border of his sanctuary, even to this mountain, which his right hand had purchased. 55 He cast out the heathen also before them, and divided them an inheritance by line, and made the tribes of Israel to dwell in their tents. Moses dies in the land of Moab & only see's the promise land with his eyes. This was a punishment for Moses because the Israelites provoked him to speak unadvisedly at the waters of strife.*

PSALMS 106:32

> *They angered him also at the waters of strife, so that it went ill with Moses for their sakes: 33 Because they provoked his spirit, so thathe spake unadvisedly with his lips. Yahushi (Joshua), Mose's servant leads the people into the promise land and they move most of the inhabitants out and took over the established land and dwellings. (Read book of Joshua)*

PSALMS 44:1

We have heard with our ears, O Alahym, our fathers have told us, what work thou didst in their days, in the times of old. 2 How thou didst drive out the heathen with thy hand, and plantedst them; how thou didst afflict the people, and cast them out. 3 For they got not the land in possession by their own sword, neither did their own arm save them: but thy right hand, and thine arm, and the light of thy countenance, because thou hadst a favour unto them. Yahushi was faithful and diligent. He helped established the Israelites in the land of Canaan and divided the land amongst the 12 Tribes. Before dying, Yahushi summaries the events past and also warns the Israelites concerning breaking Yah's covenant.

JOSHUA 23:1

And it came to pass a long time after that 𐤉𐤄𐤅𐤄 had given rest unto Israel from all their enemies round about, that Joshua waxed old [and] stricken in age. 2 And Joshua called for all Israel, [and] for their elders, and for their heads, and for their judges, and for their officers, and said unto them, I am old [and] stricken in age:3 And ye have seen all that יהוה your Alahym hath done unto all these nations because of you; for יהוה your Alahym [is] he that hath fought for you. 4 Behold, I have divided unto you by lot these nations that remain, to be an inheritance for your tribes, from Jordan, with all the nations that I have cut off, even unto the great sea westward. 5 And יהוה your Alahym, he shall expel them from before you, and drive them from out of your sight; and ye shall possess their land, as יהוה your Alahym hath promised unto you.

JOSHUA'S WARNING TO KEEP YAH'S COVENANT

6 Be ye therefore very courageous to keep and to do all that is written in the book of the law of Moses, that ye turn not aside therefrom [to] the right hand or [to] the left; 7 That ye come not among these nations, these that remain among you; neither make mention of the name of their Alahym, nor cause to swear [by them], neither serve them, nor bow yourselves unto them: 8 But cleave unto 𐤉𐤄𐤅𐤄 your Alahym, as ye have done unto this day. 9 For 𐤉𐤄𐤅𐤄 hath driven out from before you great nations and strong: but [as for] you, no man hath been able to stand before you unto this day. 10 One man of you shall chase a thousand: for 𐤉𐤄𐤅𐤄 your Alahym, he [it is] that fighteth for you, as he hath promised you. 11 Take good heed therefore unto yourselves, that ye love 𐤉𐤄𐤅𐤄 your Alahym. 12 Else if ye do in any wise go back, and cleave unto the remnant of these nations, [even] these that remain among you, and shall make marriages with them, and go in unto them, and they to you: 13 Know for a certainty that 𐤉𐤄𐤅𐤄 your Alahym will no more drive out [any of] these nations from before you; but they shall be snares and traps unto you, and scourges in your sides, and thorns in your eyes, until ye perish from off this good land which 𐤉𐤄𐤅𐤄 *your Alahym hath given you. 14 And, behold, this day I [am] going the way of all the earth: and ye know in all your hearts and in all your souls, that not one thing hath failed of all the good things which* 𐤉𐤄𐤅𐤄 *your Alahym spake concerning you; all are come to pass unto you, [and] not one thing hath failed thereof. 15 Therefore it shall come to pass, [that] as all good things are come upon you, which* 𐤉𐤄𐤅𐤄 *your Alahym promised you; so shall* 𐤉𐤄𐤅𐤄 *bring upon you all evil things, until he have destroyed you from off this good land which* 𐤉𐤄𐤅𐤄 *your Alahym hath given you. 16 When ye have transgressed the covenant of* 𐤉𐤄𐤅𐤄 *your Alahym, which he commanded you, and have gone and served other Alahym, and bowed yourselves to them; then shall the anger of* 𐤉𐤄𐤅𐤄 *be kindled against you, and ye shall perish quickly from off the good land which he hath given unto you.*

JOSHUA 24:

13.And I have given you a land for which ye did not labour, and cities which ye built not, and ye dwell in them; of the vineyards and oliveyards which ye planted not do ye eat. 14 Now therefore fear הוהי, and serve him in sincerity and in truth: and put away the Alahym which your fathers served on the other side of the flood, and in Egypt; and serve ye הוהי.15 And if it seem evil unto you to serve הוהי, choose you this day whom ye will serve; whether the Alahym which your fathers served that [were] onthe other side of the flood, or the Alahym of the Amorites, in whose land ye dwell:but as for me and my house, we will serve הוהי.16 And the people answered and said, far be it from us that we should forsake הוהי, to serve other Alahym;17 For הוהי our Alahym, he [it is] that brought us up and our fathers out of the land of Egypt, from the house of bondage, and which did those great signs in our sight, and preserved us in all the way wherein we went, and among all the people through whom we passed: 18 And הוהי drave out from before us all the people, even the Amorites which dwelt in the land: [therefore] will we also serve 𐤉𐤄𐤅𐤄*; for he [is] our Alahym. 19 And Joshua said unto the people, Ye cannot serve* 𐤉𐤄𐤅𐤄*: for he [is] a set-apart Alahym; he [is] a jealous Alahym; he will not forgive your transgressions nor your sins. 20 If ye forsake* 𐤉𐤄𐤅𐤄*, and serve strange Alahym, then he will turn and do you hurt, and consume you, after that he hath done you good. 21 And the people said unto Joshua, Nay; but we will serve* 𐤉𐤄𐤅𐤄*. 22 And Joshua said unto the people, Ye [are] witnesses against yourselves that ye have chosen you* 𐤉𐤄𐤅𐤄*, to serve him. And they said, [We are] witnesses. 23 Now therefore put away, [said he], the strange Alahym which [are] among you, and incline your heart unto* 𐤉𐤄𐤅𐤄 *Alahym of Israel. 24 And the people said unto Joshua,* 𐤉𐤄𐤅𐤄 *our Alahym will we serve, and his voice will we obey.*

JOSHUA & THE ISRAELITES CONFIRM THE COVENANT TO WORSHIP YAH

JOSHUA 24:25

So Joshua made a covenant with the people that day, and set them a statute and an ordinance in Shechem. 26 And Joshua wrote these words in the book

> *of the law of Alahym, and took a great stone, and set it up there under an oak, that [was] by the sanctuary of יהוה.*
>
> *27 And Joshua said unto all the people, Behold, this stone shall be a witness unto us; for it hath heard all the words of יהוה which he spake unto us: it shall be therefore a witness unto you, lest ye deny your Alahym.*

Now you have received the history of the children of Yeshar'Al & how the children of Yeshar'Al are required to keep the covenant, which are the commandments from יהוה writing in the first 5 books of the bible.

Now you will learn what happened to the children of Yeshar'Al when they broke the covenant and disobeyed יהוה

Back to "Egypt" Again

Egypt is another way of saying "slavery". To the Israelites, Egypt symbolizes slavery. 𐤉𐤄𐤅𐤄 warned the children of Yeshar'Al that if they broke the covenant they would return to Egypt.

DEUTERONOMY 28

> *68And 𐤉𐤄𐤅𐤄 shall bring thee into Egypt again with ships, by the way whereof I spake unto thee, Thou shalt see it no more again: and there ye shall be sold unto your enemies for bondmen and bondwomen, and no man shall buy you.*

The children of Yeshar'Al went back to "Egypt" over and over, never truly learning their lesson.

JUDGES 2:

> *7And the people served 𐤉𐤄𐤅𐤄 all the days of Joshua, and all the days of the elders that outlived Joshua, who had seen all the great works of 𐤉𐤄𐤅𐤄, that he did for Israel. 8And Joshua the son of Nun, the servant of 𐤉𐤄𐤅𐤄, died, being an hundred and ten years old. 9And they buried him in the border of his*

inheritance in Timnathheres, in the mount of Ephraim, on the north side of the hill Gaash. 10And also all that generation were gathered unto their fathers: and there arose another generation after them, which knew not יהוה, nor yet the works which he had done for Israel.

Israel's Unfaithfulness

11And the children of Israel did evil in the sight of יהוה, and served Baalim: 12And they forsook יהוה Alah of their fathers, which brought them out of the land of Egypt, and followed other gods, of the gods of the people that were round about them, and bowed themselves unto them, and provoked יהוה to anger. 13And they forsook יהוה, and served Baal and Ashtaroth. 14And the anger of יהוה was hot against Israel, and he delivered them into the hands of spoilers that spoiled them, and he sold them into the hands of their enemies round about, so that they could not any longer stand before their enemies. 15Whithersoever they went out, the hand of יהוה

was against them for evil, as 𐤉𐤄𐤅𐤄 had said, and as 𐤉𐤄𐤅𐤄 had sworn unto them: and they were greatly distressed.

Judges Raised Up

16Nevertheless 𐤉𐤄𐤅𐤄 raised up judges, which delivered them out of the hand of those that spoiled them. 17And yet they would not hearken unto their judges, but they went a whoring after other gods, and bowed themselves unto them: they turned quickly out of the way which their fathers walked in, obeying the commandments of 𐤉𐤄𐤅𐤄; but they did not so. 18And when 𐤉𐤄𐤅𐤄 raised them up judges, then 𐤉𐤄𐤅𐤄 was with the judge, and delivered them out of the hand of their enemies all the days of the judge: for it repented 𐤉𐤄𐤅𐤄 because of their groanings by reason of them that oppressed them and vexed them. 19And it came to pass, when the judge was dead, that they returned, and corrupted themselves more than their fathers, in following other gods to serve them, and to bow down unto them; they

> ceased not from their own doings, nor from their stubborn way. 20And the anger 𐤉𐤄𐤅𐤄 was hot against Israel; and he said, Because that this people hath transgressed my covenant which I commanded their fathers, and have not hearkened unto my voice; 21I also will not henceforth drive out any from before them of the nations which Joshua left when he died: 22That through them I may prove Israel, whether they will keep the way of 𐤉𐤄𐤅𐤄 to walk therein, as their fathers did keep it, or not. 23Therefore 𐤉𐤄𐤅𐤄 left those nations, without driving them out hastily; neither delivered he them into the hand of Joshua.

The children of Yeshar'Al required a King

The children of Yeshar'Al wanted to be like the other nations, which 𐤉𐤄𐤅𐤄 warned not to follow. They even demanded a king. This was a great insult to Moses because 𐤉𐤄𐤅𐤄 was their king. Although, Moses protested, 𐤉𐤄𐤅𐤄 allowed this request with this warning.

1 SAMUEL 8:

> 4Then all the elders of Israel gathered themselves together, and

came to Samuel unto Ramah, 5And said unto him, Behold, thou art old, and thy sons walk not in thy ways: now make us a king to judge us like all the nations. 6But the thing displeased Samuel, when they said, Give us a king to judge us. And Samuel prayed unto יהוה. 7And יהוה said unto Samuel, Hearken unto the voice of the people in all that they say unto thee: for they have not rejected thee, but they have rejected me, that I should not reign over them. 8According to all the works which they have done since the day that I brought them up out of Egypt even unto this day, wherewith they have forsaken me, and served other gods, so do they also unto thee. 9Now therefore hearken unto their voice: howbeit yet protest solemnly unto them, and shew them the manner of the king that shall reign over them.

Samuel's Warning About Kings

10And Samuel told all the words of יהוה unto the people that asked of him a king. 11And he said, This will be the manner of the king that shall reign over you: He will take your sons, and appoint them for himself, for his chariots, and to be his horsemen; and some shall run before his chariots. 12And he will appoint him captains over thousands, and captains over fifties; and will set them to ear his ground, and to reap his harvest, and to make his instruments of war, and instruments of his chariots. 13And he will take your daughters to be confectionaries, and to be cooks, and to be bakers. 14And he will take your fields, and your vineyards, and your oliveyards, even the best of them, and give them to his servants. 15And he will take the tenth of your seed, and of your vineyards, and give to his officers, and to his servants. 16And he will take your menservants, and your maidservants, and your goodliest young men, and your asses, and put them to his work. 17He will take the tenth of your sheep: and ye shall be his servants. 18And ye shall cry out in that day because of your king which ye shall have

> *chosen you; and 𐤉𐤄𐤅𐤄 will not hear you in that day.*

𐤉𐤄𐤅𐤄 Grants the Request

> *19 Nevertheless the people refused to obey the voice of Samuel; and they said, Nay; but we will have a king over us; 20 That we also may be like all the nations; and that our king may judge us, and go out before us, and fight our battles. 21 And Samuel heard all the words of the people, and he rehearsed them in the ears of 𐤉𐤄𐤅𐤄. 22 And 𐤉𐤄𐤅𐤄 said to Samuel, Hearken unto their voice, and make them a king. And Samuel said unto the men of Israel, Go ye every man unto his city.*

Of course, the children of Yeshar'Al did not take heed to the warning and kings ruled over them from this point onward. When the king was righteous, the people were righteous. When the king was wicked, the people were wicked.

1 SAMUEL 12:

> *12 And when ye saw that Nahash the king of the children of Ammon came against you, ye said unto me, Nay; but a king shall reign over us: when 𐤉𐤄𐤅𐤄 your Alah was your*

king. 13Now therefore behold the king whom ye have chosen, and whom ye have desired! and, behold, יהוה hath set a king over you. 14If ye will fear יהוה, and serve him, and obey his voice, and not rebel against the commandment of יהוה, then shall both ye and also the king that reigneth over you continue following יהוה your Alah: 15But if ye will not obey the voice of יהוה, but rebel against the commandment of יהוה, then shall the hand of יהוה be against you, as it was against your fathers. 16Now therefore stand and see this great thing, which יהוה will do before your eyes. 17Is it not wheat harvest to day? I will call unto יהוה, and he shall send thunder and rain; that ye may perceive and see that your wickedness is great, which ye have done in the sight of יהוה, in asking you a king. 18So Samuel called unto יהוה; and יהוה sent thunder and rain that day: and all the people greatly feared יהוה and Samuel.

19And all the people said unto Samuel, Pray for thy servants unto

יהוה thy Alah, that we die not: for we have added unto all our sins this evil, to ask us a king. 20And Samuel said unto the people, Fear not: ye have done all this wickedness: yet turn not aside from following יהוה, but serve יהוה with all your heart; 21And turn ye not aside: for then should ye go after vain things, which cannot profit nor deliver; for they are vain. 22For יהוה will not forsake his people for his great name's sake: because it hath pleased יהוה to make you his people. 23Moreover as for me, forbid that I should sin against יהוה in ceasing to pray for you: but I will teach you the good and the right way: 24Only fear יהוה, and serve him in truth with all your heart: for consider how great things he hath done for you. 25But if ye shall still do wickedly, ye shall be consumed, both ye and your king.

PSALMS 106:

Many times did he deliver them; but they provoked him with their counsel, and were brought low for their iniquity.

PSALMS 81:

8Hear, O my people, and I will testify unto thee: O Israel, if thou wilt hearken unto me;

9There shall no strange god be in thee; neither shalt thou worship any strange god.

10I am יהוה thy Alah, which brought thee out of the land of Egypt: open thy mouth wide, and I will fill it.

11But my people would not hearken to my voice; and Israel would none of me.

12So I gave them up unto their own hearts' lust: and they walked in their own counsels.

13Oh that my people had hearkened unto me, and Israel had walked in my ways!

14I should soon have subdued their enemies, and turned my hand against their adversaries.

> 15The haters of 𐤉𐤄𐤅𐤄 should have
> submitted themselves unto him:
> but their time should have endured
> for ever.
>
> 16He should have fed them also
> with the finest of the wheat: and
> with honey out of the rock should I
> have satisfied thee.

ISAIAH 30:9

> That this is a rebellious people,
> lying children, children that will
> not hear the law of 𐤉𐤄𐤅𐤄:

ISAIAH 65:2

> I have spread out my hands all the
> day unto a rebellious people, which
> walketh in a way that was not
> good, after their own thoughts;

I am not going to review all the kings of the children of Yeshar'Al, however, I will give this summary.

Saul was the first official king of the children of Yeshar'Al. He did evil in the sight of 𐤉𐤄𐤅𐤄 and before he even died, 𐤉𐤄𐤅𐤄 anointed a new king over the children of Yeshar'Al, that being David. David was a righteous king whom 𐤉𐤄𐤅𐤄 loved, however, he was not perfect. He committed adultery and this caused his kingdom to fall. A curse then upon his family, likely still on his family 'til this day. There was much family drama in David's life - from infant death, incest, adultery, murder, betrayal and more. When his son took rulership the kingdom of Yeshar'Al was split into two. One called "the Kingdom of Judah" and the other, "The Kingdom of Israel". The kingdom of Israel had no righteous king and they were the first to scatter.

Jeroboam was the first, but not last wicked king of Yeshar'Al

1 KINGS 12:

> *28Whereupon the king took counsel, and made two calves of gold, and said unto them, It is too much for you to go up to Jerusalem: behold thy gods, O Israel, which brought thee up out of the land of Egypt. 29And he set the one in Bethel, and the other put he in Dan. 30And this thing became a sin: for the people went to worship before the one, even unto Dan. 31And he made an house of high places, and made priests of the lowest of the people, which were not of the sons of Levi.*

While the kingdom of Judah was far from perfect, many kings have been righteous and led the people to righteousness. Unfortunately, it was not enough and the curse of Deuteronomy 28 could not be held because the kings were not always perfect.

The Last Righteous King of Judah

2 KINGS 23:

> 24Moreover the workers with familiar spirits, and the wizards, and the images, and the idols, and all the abominations that were spied in the land of Judah and in Jerusalem, did Josiah put away, that he might perform the words of the law which were written in the book that Hilkiah the priest found in the house of 𐤉𐤄𐤅𐤄. 25And like unto him was there no king before him, that turned to 𐤉𐤄𐤅𐤄 with all his heart, and with all his soul, and with all his might, according to all the law of Moses; neither after him arose there any like him.
>
> 26Notwithstanding 𐤉𐤄𐤅𐤄 turned not from the fierceness of his great wrath, wherewith his anger was kindled against Judah, because of all the provocations that Manasseh had provoked him withal. 27And 𐤉𐤄𐤅𐤄 said, I will remove Judah also

> *out of my sight, as I have removed*
> *Israel, and will cast off this city*
> *Jerusalem which I have chosen, and*
> *the house of which I said, My name*
> *shall be there.*

We are living in the curse of Deuteronomy as of today.

יהוה will Gather his people & Plead with them

PROVERBS 3:11

My son, despise not the chastening of יהוה; neither be weary of his correction:12For whom יהוה loveth he correcteth; even as a father the son in whom he delighteth.

EZEKIEL 34:11-13

11For thus saith Master יהוה; Behold, I, even I, will both search my sheep, and seek them out. 12As a shepherd seeketh out his flock in the day that he is among his sheep that are scattered; so will I seek out my sheep, and will deliver them out of all places where they have been scattered in the cloudy and dark day. 13And I will bring them out from the people, and gather them from the countries, and will bring them to their own land, and feed them upon the mountains of Israel by the rivers, and in all the inhabited places of the country. 14I will feed them in a good pasture, and upon the high mountains of Israel shall their fold be: there shall they lie in a good fold, and in a fat pasture shall they feed upon the mountains of Israel. 15I will feed my flock, and I will cause them to lie down, saith Master 𐤉𐤄𐤅𐤄. 16I will seek that which was lost, and bring again that which was driven away, and will bind up that which was broken, and will strengthen that which was sick: but I will destroy the fat and the strong; I will feed them with judgment.

17And as for you, O my flock, thus saith Master 𐤉𐤄𐤅𐤄; Behold, I judge between cattle and cattle, between the rams and the he goats. 18Seemeth it a small thing unto you to have eaten up the good pasture, but ye must tread down with your feet the residue of your pastures? and to have drunk of the deep waters, but ye must foul the residue with your feet? 19And as for my flock, they eat that which ye have trodden with your feet; and they drink that which ye have fouled with your feet.

20Therefore thus saith Master 𐤉𐤄𐤅𐤄 unto them; Behold, I, even I, will judge between the fat cattle and between the lean cattle. 21Because ye have thrust with side and with shoulder, and pushed all the diseased with your horns, till ye have scattered them abroad; 22Therefore will I save my flock, and they shall no more be a prey; and I will judge between cattle and cattle.

23And I will set up one shepherd over them, and he shall feed them, even my servant David; he shall feed them, and he shall be their shepherd. 24And I יהוה will be their Alah, and my servant David a prince among them; I יהוה have spoken it.

25And I will make with them a covenant of peace, and will cause the evil beasts to cease out of the land: and they shall dwell safely in the wilderness, and sleep in the woods. 26And I will make them and the places round about my hill a blessing; and I will cause the shower to come down in his season; there shall be showers of blessing. 27And the tree of the field shall yield her fruit, and the earth shall yield her increase, and they shall be safe in their land, and shall know that I am יהוה, when I have broken the bands of their yoke, and delivered them out of the hand of those that served themselves of them. 28And they shall no more be a prey to the heathen, neither shall the beast of the land devour them; but they shall dwell safely, and none shall make them afraid. 29And I will raise up for them a plant of renown, and they shall be no more consumed with hunger in the land, neither bear the shame of the heathen any more. 30Thus shall they know that I יהוה their Alah am with them, and that they, even the house of Israel, are my people, saith Master יהוה. 31And ye my flock, the flock of my pasture, are men, and I am your Alah, saith Master יהוה.

HOSEA 13:4, 9

4Yet I am יהוה thy Alah from the land of Egypt, and thou shalt know no Alah but me: for there is no saviour beside me.

9O Israel, thou hast destroyed thyself; but in me is thine help.

ISAIAH 11:11

11And it shall come to pass in that day, that יהוה shall set his hand again the second time to recover the remnant of his people, which shall be left, from Assyria, and from Egypt, and from Pathros, and from Cush, and from Elam, and from Shinar, and from Hamath, and from the islands of the sea.

12.*And he shall set up an ensign for the nations, and shall assemble the outcasts of Israel, and gather together the dispersed of Judah from the four corners of the earth.*

The Consequences of Not Returning to 𐤉𐤄𐤅𐤄

Those 𐤉𐤄𐤅𐤄 loves, he punishes

Amos 3:2

"You only have I chosen of all the families of the earth; therefore I will punish you for all your sins."

Proverbs 28:2, 9

2For the transgression of a land many are the princes thereof: but by a man of understanding and knowledge the state thereof shall be prolonged.

9He that turneth away his ear from hearing the law, even his prayer shall be abomination.

Proverbs 13:19

The desire accomplished is sweet to the soul: but it is abomination to fools to depart from evil.

EZEKIEL 18:4

Behold, all souls are mine; as the soul of the father, so also the soul of the son is mine: the soul that sinneth, it shall die.

PSALMS 11:6

On the wicked He will rain down fiery coals and sulfur; a scorching wind will be their portion.

MALACHI 4:1-3

1 "For behold, the day is coming, burning like a furnace, when all the arrogant and every evildoer will be stubble; the day is coming when I will set them ablaze," says 𐤉𐤄𐤅𐤄 of Hosts. "Not a root or branch will be left to them."

2 "But for you who fear My name, the sun of righteousness will rise with healing in its wings, and you will go out and leap like calves from the stall. 3 Then you will trample the wicked, for they will be ashes under the soles of your feet on the day I am preparing," says 𐤉𐤄𐤅𐤄 of Hosts.

ISAIAH 65:11-12

11But ye are they that forsake יהוה, that forget my holy mountain, that prepare a table for that troop, and that furnish the drink offering unto that number.

12Therefore will I number you to the sword, and ye shall all bow down to the slaughter: because when I called, ye did not answer; when I spake, ye did not hear; but did evil before mine eyes, and did choose that wherein I delighted not.

Do you want the Curse of Deuteronomy to come back on us again?
ISAIAH 65:13-15

13Therefore thus saith Master יהוה, Behold, my servants shall eat, but ye shall be hungry: behold, my servants shall drink, but ye shall be thirsty: behold, my servants shall rejoice, but ye shall be ashamed:

14Behold, my servants shall sing for joy of heart, but ye shall cry for sorrow of heart, and shall howl for vexation of spirit.

15And ye shall leave your name for a curse unto my chosen: for Master

*𐤉𐤄𐤅𐤄 shall slay thee, and **call his servants by another name:***

The rebellious children of Yeshar'Al are the Suffering Servants of Isaiah 53

The Wicked are a Randsom

PROVERBS 21:18

The wicked shall be a ransom for the righteous, and the transgressor for the upright.

The unrighteous are a target for the Curse of Deuteronomy 28.

There are different doctrines being professed in the bible. One is punishing the wicked for their own sins and the other is punishing the innocent for the sins of others.

> OLD TESTAMENT =
> WICKED ARE RANSOM
> DEATH PUNISHMENT OF WICKED TO
> SAVE EVERYONE
>
> NEW TESTAMENT =
> INNOCENT ARE RANSOM
> HUMAN SACRIFICE OF INNOCENT TO
> SAVE EVERYONE

Which one is Righteous?

Which one do you think the New Testament speaks about?

Human sacrificing for sin is illegal and against the Torah law of the bible, but the Pagans wrote the New Testament, that's why its not found in Hebrew/Manakahthey. The original manuscripts of the new testament were written in Greek. The Greek pagans believed in human sacrifice for sins, especially that of the innocent. This is why Jesus is heavily pushed. Those of the children of Yeshar'Al who wicked left 𐤉𐤄𐤅𐤄 to follow the other nations believed in sacrificing an innocent to save yourself. The reason for this is because it was easier to contemplate then believing you would be punished for your sins.

𐤉𐤄𐤅𐤄 does not save the wicked by killing someone innocent, that isn't justice. Justice is executing righteous judgment and you should not need to be told that killing someone innocent isn't righteous. Jesus never saved any black person from slavery nor did he stop the curse of Deuteronomy. Who did Jesus save?

If Jesus is your savior why don't you ask him to stop the police from killing Black people. 𐤉𐤄𐤅𐤄 is allowing the curse to go on the rebellious ones from amongst us, you only need to return to him to escape the curse.

Proverbs 1:23-25

23Turn you at my reproof: behold, I will pour out my spirit unto you, I will make known my words unto you.

24Because I have called, and ye refused; I have stretched out my hand, and no man regarded;

25But ye have set at nought all my counsel, and would none of my reproof:

Isaiah 59:2

But your iniquities have separated between you and your Alah, and your sins have hid his face from you, that he will not hear.

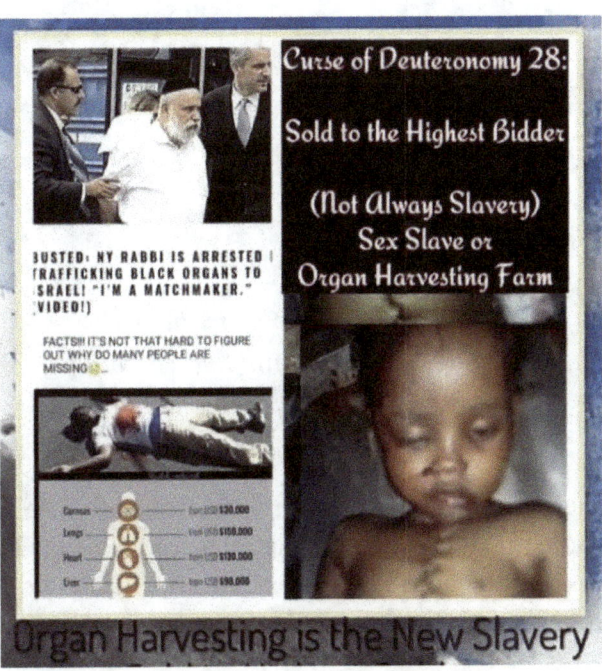
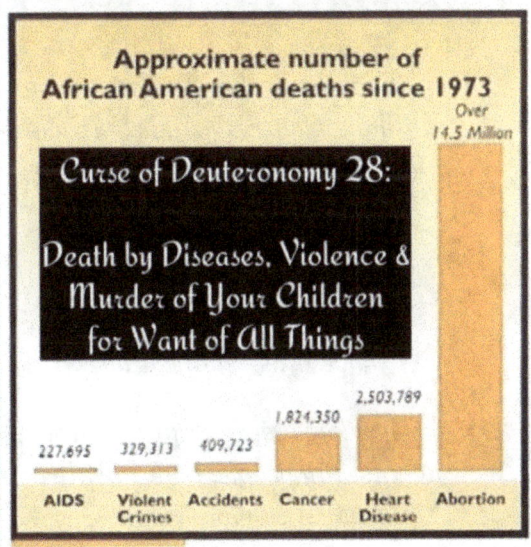

The Nations will be Visited & Punished

GENESIS 12:3

> *3And I will bless them that bless thee, and curse him that curseth thee: and in thee shall all families of the earth be blessed.*

The children of Yeshar'Al received the promise of Abraham. The way other nations are blessed is by blessing the house of Yeshar'Al. Those that cursed us, will surely be cursed also.

PSALMS 83:

> *1{A Song or Psalm of Asaph.} Keep not thou silence, O Alaheym: hold not thy peace, and be not still, O Al.*
>
> *2For, lo, thine enemies make a tumult: and they that hate thee have lifted up the head.*
>
> *3They have taken crafty counsel against thy people, and consulted against thy hidden ones.*

4They have said, Come, and let us cut them off from being a nation; that the name of Israel may be no more in remembrance.

5For they have consulted together with one consent: they are confederate against thee:

6The tabernacles of Edom, and the Ishmaelites; of Moab, and the Hagarenes;

7Gebal, and Ammon, and Amalek; the Philistines with the inhabitants of Tyre;

8Assur also is joined with them: they have holpen the children of Lot. Selah.

The nations who caused the children of Yeshar'Al to lose their identity will be cursed. Imagine how all the curses in Deuteronomy came upon 𐤉𐤄𐤅𐤄 (Yahuah's), chosen people, and what will happen to the nations which he didn't even know.

ZECHARIAH 9:13

When I have bent Judah for me, filled the bow with Ephraim, and raised up thy sons, O Zion, against thy sons, O

Greece, and made thee as the sword of a mighty man.

ISAIAH 60:12-14

12For the nation and kingdom that will not serve thee shall perish; yea, those nations shall be utterly wasted.

13The glory of Lebanon shall come unto thee, the fir tree, the pine tree, and the box together, to beautify the place of my sanctuary; and I will make the place of my feet glorious.

14The sons also of them that afflicted thee shall come bending unto thee; and all they that despised thee shall bow themselves down at the soles of thy feet; and they shall call thee, The city of 𐤉𐤄𐤅𐤄, The Zion of the Holy One of Israel.

PSALMS 58:10-11

10The righteous shall rejoice when he seeth the vengeance: he shall wash his feet in the blood of the wicked.

11So that a man shall say, Verily there is a reward for the righteous: verily he is a Alah that judgeth in the earth.

DEUTERONOMY 32:42-43

42I will make mine arrows drunk with blood, and my sword shall devour flesh; and that with the blood of the slain and of the captives, from the beginning of revenges upon the enemy.

43Rejoice, O ye nations, with his people: for he will avenge the blood of his servants, and will render vengeance to his adversaries, and will be merciful unto his land, and to his people.

"For the white man to ask the black man if he hates him is just like the rapist asking the raped, or the wolf asking the sheep, 'Do you hate me?' The white man is in no moral position to accuse anyone else of hate! Why, when all of my ancestors are snake-bitten, and I'm snake-bitten, and I warn my children to avoid snakes, what does that snake sound like accusing me of hate-teaching?"

Glory & No more Tears

This section is the future prophesies of what is known as "the Kingdom". The kingdom is a time, not place, when the Children of Yeshar'Al will be in rulership. This period of rulership will be forever. We will be saved from the curses of Deuteronomy 28:15-68 and we will instead receive the privileges written in

DEUTERONOMY 28:1-14

1And it shall come to pass, if thou shalt hearken diligently unto the voice of ᛭ᛉᛉ᛭ your Alah, to observe and to do all his commandments which I command thee this day, that ᛭ᛉᛉ᛭ your Alah will set thee on high above all nations of the earth: 2And all these blessings shall come on thee, and

overtake thee, if thou shalt hearken unto the voice of יהוה your Alah.

3Blessed shalt thou be in the city, and blessed shalt thou be in the field.

4Blessed shall be the fruit of thy body, and the fruit of thy ground, and the fruit of thy cattle, the increase of thy kine, and the flocks of thy sheep.

5Blessed shall be thy basket and thy store.

6Blessed shalt thou be when thou comest in, and blessed shalt thou be when thou goest out.

7יהוה shall cause thine enemies that rise up against thee to be smitten before thy face: they shall come out against thee one way, and flee before thee seven ways. 8יהוה shall command the blessing upon thee in thy storehouses, and in all that thou settest thine hand unto; and he shall bless thee in the land which יהוה your Alah giveth thee. 9יהוה shall establish thee an holy people unto himself, as he hath sworn unto thee, if thou shalt keep the commandments of יהוה your Alah, and walk in his ways. 10And all people of the earth shall see that thou art called by the name of יהוה; and they shall be afraid of thee. 11 And 𐤉𐤄𐤅𐤄 shall make thee plenteous in goods, in the fruit of thy body, and in the fruit of thy cattle, and in the fruit of thy ground, in the land which 𐤉𐤄𐤅𐤄 sware unto thy fathers to give thee. 12 𐤉𐤄𐤅𐤄 shall open unto thee his good treasure, the heaven to give the rain unto thy land in his season, and to bless all the work of thine hand: and thou shalt lend unto many nations, and thou shalt not borrow. 13 And 𐤉𐤄𐤅𐤄 shall make thee the head, and not the tail; and thou shalt be above only, and thou shalt not be beneath; if that thou hearken unto the commandments of 𐤉𐤄𐤅𐤄 your Alah, which I command thee this day, to observe and to do them: 14 And thou shalt not go aside from any of the words which I command thee this day, to the right hand, or to the left, to go after other Alahs to serve them.

These are the Privileges of Serving 𐤉𐤄𐤅𐤄 and Keeping the Torah

ISAIAH 61:9-10

9 And their seed shall be known among the Gentiles, and their offspring among the people: all that see

them shall acknowledge them, that they are the seed which 𐤉𐤄𐤅𐤄 hath blessed.

10 I will greatly rejoice in 𐤉𐤄𐤅𐤄, my soul shall be joyful in my Elohim; for he hath clothed me with the garments of salvation, he hath covered me with the robe of righteousness, as a bridegroom decketh himself with ornaments, and as a bride adorneth herself with her jewels.

ISAIAH 26:1

In that day shall this song be sung in the land of Judah; We have a strong city; salvation will Elohim appoint for walls and bulwarks. 2 Open ye the gates, that the righteous nation which keepeth the truth may enter in.

THE LOOK OF NEW JERUSALEM

DANIEL 2:44

And in the days of these kings shall the Elohim of heaven set up a kingdom, which shall never be destroyed: and the kingdom shall not be left to other people, but it shall break in pieces and consume all these kingdoms, and it shall stand for ever.

ISAIAH 60:1-6 & 17-22

(1-6) 1 Arise, shine; for thy light is come, and the glory of יהוה is risen upon thee. 2 For, behold, the darkness shall cover the earth, and gross darkness the people: but יהוה shall arise upon thee, and his glory shall be seen upon thee. 3 And the Gentiles shall come to thy light, and kings to the brightness of thy rising. 4 Lift up thine eyes round about, and see: all they gather themselves together, they come to thee: thy sons shall come from far, and thy daughters shall be nursed at thy side. 5 Then thou shalt see, and flow together, and thine heart shall fear, and be enlarged; because the abundance of the sea shall be converted unto thee, the forces of the Gentiles shall come unto thee. 6 The multitude of camels shall cover thee, the dromedaries of Midian and Ephah; all they from Sheba shall come: they shall bring gold and incense; and they shall shew forth the praises of יהוה.

(17-22) 17 For brass I will bring gold, and for iron I will bring silver, and for wood brass, and for stones iron: I will also make thy officers peace, and thine exactors righteousness. 18 Violence shall no

more be heard in thy land, wasting nor destruction within thy borders; but thou shalt call thy walls Salvation, and thy gates Praise. 19 The sun shall be no more thy light by day; neither for brightness shall the moon give light unto thee: but 𐤉𐤄𐤅𐤄 shall be unto thee an everlasting light, and thy Elohim thy glory. 20 Thy sun shall no more go down; neither shall thy moon withdraw itself: for 𐤉𐤄𐤅𐤄 shall be thine everlasting light, and the days of thy mourning shall be ended.

NO MORE WARS

MICAH 4:3

And he shall judge among many people, and rebuke strong nations afar off; and they shall beat their swords into plowshares, and their spears into pruninghooks: nation shall not lift up a sword against nation, neither shall they learn war any more.

EZEKIEL 36:33-38 -33

Thus saith the Sovereign 𐤉𐤄𐤅𐤄; In the day that I shall have cleansed you from all your iniquities I will also cause you to dwell in the cities, and the wastes shall be builded. 34 And the desolate land shall be tilled, whereas it lay desolate in the sight of all that passed by. 35 And they shall say, This land that was desolate is become like the garden of Eden; and the waste and desolate and ruined cities are become fenced, and are inhabited. 36 Then the heathen that are left round about you shall know that I יהוה build the ruined places, and plant that that was desolate: I יהוה have spoken it, and I will do it. 37 Thus saith the Sovereign יהוה; I will yet for this be inquired of by the house of Israel, to do it for them; I will increase them with men like a flock. 38 As the set-apart flock, as the flock of Jerusalem in her solemn feasts; so shall the waste cities be filled with flocks of men: and they shall know that I am יהוה.

ISAIAH 51:3

For יהוה shall comfort Zion: he will comfort all her waste places; and he will make her wilderness like Eden, and her desert like the garden of יהוה; joy and gladness shall be found therein, thanksgiving, and the voice of melody.

NO DEATH, SORROW or PAIN

ISAIAH 25:8

He will swallow up death in victory; and the Master יהוה will wipe away tears from off all faces; and the rebuke of his people shall he take away from off all the earth: for יהוה hath spoken it.

HOSEA 13:14

I will ransom them from the power of the grave; I will redeem them from death: O death, I will be thy plagues; O grave, I will be thy destruction: repentance shall be hid from mine eyes.

NO MORE HUNGER or THIRST

ISAIAH 35:6

Then shall the lame man leap as an hart, and the tongue of the dumb sing: for in the wilderness shall waters break out, and streams in the desert. 7 And the parched ground shall become a pool, and the thirsty land springs of water: in the habitation of dragons, where each lay, shall be grass with reeds and rushes. 8 And an highway shall be there, and a way, and it shall be called The way of holiness; the unclean shall not pass over it; but it shall be for those: the wayfaring men, though fools, shall not err therein. 9 No lion shall be there, nor any ravenous beast shall go up thereon, it shall not be found there; but the redeemed shall walk there: 10 And the ransomed of 𐤉𐤄𐤅𐤄 shall return, and come to Zion with songs and everlasting joy upon their heads: they shall obtain joy and gladness, and sorrow and sighing shall flee away.

NO AGING OLD PEOPLE
ZECHARIAH 8:3

Thus saith 𐤉𐤄𐤅𐤄; I am returned unto Zion, and will dwell in the midst of Jerusalem: and Jerusalem shall be called a city of truth; and the mountain of 𐤉𐤄𐤅𐤄 of hosts the set-apart mountain. 4 Thus saith 𐤉𐤄𐤅𐤄 of hosts; There shall yet old men and old women dwell in the streets of Jerusalem, and every man with his staff in his hand for very age.

ISAIAH 65:17

For, behold, I create new heavens and a new earth: and the former shall not be remembered, nor come into mind. 18 But be ye glad and rejoice for ever in that which I create: for, behold, I create Jerusalem a rejoicing, and her people a joy. 19 And I will rejoice in Jerusalem, and joy in my people: and the voice of weeping shall be no more heard in her, nor the voice of crying. 20 There shall be no more thence an infant of days, nor an old man that hath not filled his days: for the child shall die an hundred years old; but the sinner being an hundred years old shall be accursed. 21 And they shall build houses, and inhabit them; and they shall plant vineyards, and eat the fruit of them. 22 They shall not build, and another inhabit; they shall not plant, and another eat: for as the days of a tree are the days of my people, and mine elect shall long enjoy the work of their hands. 23 They shall not labour in vain, nor bring forth for trouble; for they are the seed of the blessed of יהוה*, and their offspring with them. 24 And it shall come to pass, that before they call, I will answer; and while they are yet speaking, I will* *hear. 25 The wolf and the lamb shall feed together, and the lion shall eat straw like the bullock: and dust shall be the serpent's meat. They shall not hurt nor destroy in all my set-apart mountain, saith* יהוה.

EZEKIEL 36:33

Thus saith the Sovereign יהוה; *In the day that I shall have cleansed you from all your iniquities I will also cause you to dwell in the cities, and the wastes shall be builded. 34 And the desolate land shall be tilled, whereas it lay desolate in the sight of all that passed by. 35 And they shall say, This land that was desolate is become like the garden of Eden; and the waste and desolate and ruined cities are become fenced, and are inhabited. 36 Then the heathen that are left round about you shall know that I* יהוה *build the ruined places, and plant that that was desolate: I* יהוה *have spoken it, and I will do it. 37 Thus saith the Sovereign* יהוה; *I will yet for this be inquired of by the house of Israel, to do it for them; I will increase them with men like a flock. 38 As the set-apart flock, as the flock of Jerusalem in her solemn feasts; so shall the waste cities be filled with flocks of men: and they shall know that I am יהוה.*

SLAVERY IN THE KINGDOM

ISAIAH 14:1

For יהוה will have mercy on Jacob, and will yet choose Israel, and set them in their own land: and the strangers shall be joined with them, and they shall cleave to the house of Jacob. 2 And the people shall take them, and bring them to their place: and the house of Israel shall possess them in the land of יהוה for servants and handmaids: and they shall take them captives, whose captives they were; and they shall rule over their oppressors.

ANIMALS ARE AT PEACE
(see Vegetarian Kingdom)

ISAIAH 11:6

The wolf also shall dwell with the lamb, and the leopard shall lie down with the kid; and the calf and the young lion and the fatling together; and a little child shall lead them. 7 And the cow and the bear shall feed; their young ones shall lie down together: and the lion shall eat straw like the ox. 8 And the sucking child shall play on the hole of the asp, and the weaned child shall put his hand on the cockatrice' den. 9 They shall not hurt nor destroy in all my set-apart mountain: for the earth shall be full of the knowledge of יהוה, as the waters cover the sea.

How to Return Back to 𐤉𐤄𐤅𐤄

- Worship only 𐤉𐤄𐤅𐤄 (Yahuah)
- Pray toward Yerushalam (Jerusalem)
- Keep the Commandments of 𐤉𐤄𐤅𐤄
- Learn the language
- Embrace your Culture

Worship only 𐤉𐤄𐤅𐤄

This means to call on 𐤉𐤄𐤅𐤄 when you pray.

Pray only in his name.

Put your trust in him and <u>not man</u>

Watch out for the Pagan Israelites. A Pagan Israelite are those who claim to serve Yah yet in the same breathe praises a man. This man goes by various names such as Jesus, Yahushua, Yahawashi etc… Pagans sacrificed innocent humans for sin of the wicked. This is the foundation of Christianity, that Christ was without sin and had to die for the wicked. JC never saved any black person. Where was he when Deuteronomy was hitting the children of Yeshar'Al real hard? All Christians are Pagan & believe in human sacrifice for sins.

The truth is 𐤉𐤄𐤅𐤄 is the only one who can forgive sins. We broke our covenant with him and it is to him you ought to seek forgiveness. He said to repent and return to him. Remember, Yeshar'Al is his wife, not his sons wife. How does that sound?

Pray toward Yerushalam (Jerusalem)

When you pray to 𐤉𐤄𐤅𐤄, pray toward the land of Yerushalam.

2 Chronicles 6:

36If they sin against thee, (for there is no man which sinneth not,) and thou be angry with them, and deliver them over before their enemies, and they carry them away captives unto a land far off or near;

37Yet if they bethink themselves in the land whither they are carried captive, and turn and pray unto thee in the land of their captivity,

saying, We have sinned, we have done amiss, and have dealt wickedly; 38If they return to thee with all their heart and with all their soul in the land of their captivity, whither they have carried them captives, and pray toward their land, which thou gavest unto their fathers, and toward the city which thou hast chosen, and toward the house which I have built for thy name: 39Then hear thou from the heavens, even from thy dwelling place, their prayer and their supplications, and maintain their cause, and forgive thy people which have sinned against thee.

Keep the Commandments of 𐤉𐤄𐤅𐤄

Know where the commandments are. The commandments were given to the children of Yeshar'Al by the hand of Mashah (Moses). His books are found in the first 5 books of the bible. There are no other commandments written by Mashah (Moses). These are called the Torath, meaning "the laws".

Torah 𐤄𐤓𐤅𐤕 (Thurah) = One law

Torath 𐤕𐤓𐤅𐤕 (Thurath) = laws

DEUTERONOMY 34:10

And there arose not a prophet since in Israel like unto Mashah, whom 𐤉𐤄𐤅𐤄 knew face to face,

Learn the language

My name is Itharey and I am the one whom 𐤉𐤄𐤅𐤄 allowed to discover the Manakahthey language written in Zephaniah 3:9.

ZEPHANIAH 3:9:

9 For then will I return to the people a refined language, that they may call upon the name of 𐤉𐤄𐤅𐤄, to serve him with shoulder to shoulder,

I am the woman prophesied in Zephaniah 3:10 to bring this language. See Manakahthey.com to learn this language by signing up for the free lessons.

Hebrew came from Manakahthey. To know Ancient Hebrew is to know the origins of the symbols and it comes from hand signs. The word "Manakahthey" means "from origins of hand signs".

ZEPHANIAH 3:10

10 from beyond to river of Cush, Itharey, Daughter of the Diaspora, shall brings Manakahthey.

Common phrases

ツヰ6W (Shalum) – meaning peace

ヨ△ᗡX (Thudah) – meaning thank you

ヨᗡᗡX (Thurah) – meaning the law

Xgw (Shabath) – meaning 7th day of the week

The Language before Hebrew is called Manakahthey. Hebrew is not the returned language.

Read "Primitive Sign Language, Etymology of Ancient Biblical Hebrew". Purchase at

PrimitiveSignLanguage.com/shop

Embrace your Culture

𝕐𝕳𝖂𝕳 said not to follow the other nations, in their ways or traditions. This includes language, clothes, music and especially knowledge of 𝕐𝕳𝖂𝕳. Why would you uplift the culture of another people? Our children should be proud of who they are and our culture when it is embraced helps to teach our children who we are and that we are special.

Visit SetapartToYah.com – for clothes

Visit YahsSingles.com –

for marriage with those who call on Yah & Keep his Commandments

"The Origins and Traditions of Marriage"

For more information

There is a lot to learn. This book is an introduction for those who don't know they are the children of Yeshar'Al or for those who want to know the descendants of Yeshar'Al need to obey 𝕐𝕳𝖂𝕳.

Look for the book

"The Mini Thurath:

New Believers Guide to Keeping the Commandments"

DOWNLOAD THE APP

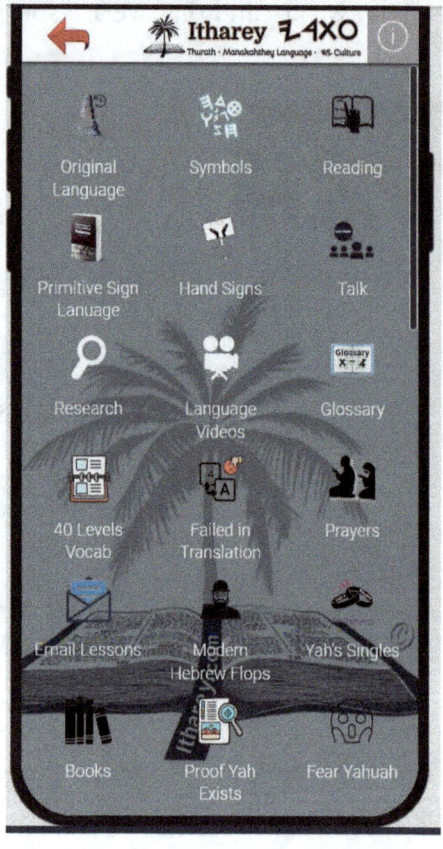

Itharey.com

www.ingramcontent.com/pod-product-compliance
Lightning Source LLC
Chambersburg PA
CBHW071854070526
44583CB00016B/1691